I0461168

The 7-Minute Shift

Get out of your own way, manifest your greatest self, and grow a massively successful business in as little as 7 minutes a day!

MICHELLE SERA

Copyright © 2022 Michelle Sera

All rights reserved. This is the sole work of the author, and no portion of this publication may be copied or re-published in any publication without express permission of the publisher or author.

Paperback
ISBN: 979-8-9869118-0-9

What others have said…

*"Just like when you speak with her in person, Michelle offers an accessible way to not only envision the life and business you want, but also make it happen. Through the stories and exercises she shares in **The 7-Minute Shift**, she makes manifesting seem less like mysterious happenstance and more like a process I am empowered to implement for welcoming alignment and wealth.*

Michelle gets my head out of a downward spiral and back in touch with my inner wisdom and strong body every time. This book is a gift in that it allows me to have her help anytime I need it."

Jessica Wright, Personal Transformation Coach

*"Michelle is gifted at helping you focus your mind and energy so you can shift your state and manifest incredible results in your business (I would know, I'm the client who created the waiting list you'll read about!) **The 7-Minute Shift** is powerful when you commit to implementing it.*

Michelle's work is something I continue to use daily as I grow my business because energy really does flow where attention goes."

Maxine Loader, 7-Figure FB Ads Strategist

"When it comes to living the principles of mindset – vibration and alignment, Michelle gets it right, 100% of the time!

This workbook is a gem of information and expertise born of experience and trust in the universal principles she generously shares with her readers. By breaking it down into simple concepts and principles, Michelle gives you the tools to create the life you want to live.

Take a look. You won't be disappointed."

Tina DeMarco, Writing coach & copywriter

"Michelle has a gift for taking ideas and methodologies and compacting these into a streamlined version of what she did to achieve results for herself and others.

In her book **The 7-Minute Shift** *you will be compelled to look within yourself and begin to explore your belief system, and mind set to learn how to raise your vibrational frequency to create the life you love with more joy, fulfillment, and abundance."*

Moira Sutton, Empowerment Life & Lifestyle Coach

Dedication

To Madelaine:

There once was a woman who had two children—the Sun and the Moon. She loved them more than the stars. The Sun always consumed her attention, it was unavoidable. At times, it blinded her. But her child, the Moon, was, in her own right, a powerful, beautiful presence that in her quiet strength, swelled the woman's heart in a way nothing else or no one else could.

She outshines them all.

I love you. I love who you are.

To Devin:

Consciousness creates itself in many forms to experience itself differently. It needs to do this to expand and grow. You are an expander. You help me experience life differently. And I am so lucky to have you. You do you and keep surprising us all.

I love you.

To Jason:

Just follow the sign for the beach, that's where we'll meet.

This is going to sound SO cliche, but here goes… Thank you for never judging me. Thank you for seeing me as someone incredible. Thank you for not expecting me to be someone I'm not. Thank you for believing in me way more than I have ever believed in myself. Thank you for letting me see the world through your eyes, it's grounding. Our long conversations fulfill me. May we never tire of portals, 16 Horsepower, and restructuring the world.

If I ever questioned what it means to be "destined"—I can say I've experienced it in you.

I love you (but you know this).

Cheers to being foodies, overthinkers, and besties.

To Tubbly:

You left in the midst of this book being created, so I capture a spark of your energy here by remembering all the time you spent curled in the crook of my folded legs, while I wrote away on the sofa. Even with the incessant rubbing of your face on my lap desk, clawing of cords, and the direct hits from kittie sneezes, I thank you for the company. I miss you. I never expected you to be the companion you became. Journey on my friend.

"Set your life on fire. Seek those who fan your flames."

—Rumi

Contents

Acknowledgements

As the "little" me said, *"this book isn't big enough for acknowledgements,"* I had an immediate sensation of being smacked on the forehead. There are so many people who helped me get this done. In ways most of which you probably aren't even aware of.

First, let me say that I am in appreciation of my family for everything they have given, taught, and sacrificed. Thank you.

And second, if you're ever so lucky to find a small group of people who light up your life and instantly evoke a smile from your face…tell them. Hold space for them in honor of their bliss-filled, mind-blowing, epiphany-inducing selves.

Know that you manifested them and they, you. Not everyone can say they have a true High Vibe Tribe that helps them reach for even higher vibrations and understandings of the Universe and Self (is there a difference?).

Thank you, High Vibe Tribe: Kent, Melissa, Miguel, Tracy, and Miriam. Each of you unknowingly contributed to the clarity, happiness, and belief required to write this book. With your laughter, desire for fun, dancing, deep insights, reframing, and relentless pursuit of something MORE…I discovered that even surrender has company.

Much love.

Thank you, Chris, for being a true inspiration, level sounding board, and friend. Thank you for your unending support, hours of conversation, and ability to make me think. In alignment, we proceed. There are still infinite quantum leaps to be had. *You are a powerful creator.*

And finally, thank you George. I suppose patience is inherent in an editor. At least it is in you, and I SO appreciate your kindness, support, and guidance in getting this book done. May there be many more :)

Foreword

In 2016, I received an email from a friend introducing me to a lady whom she felt I needed to know. *My friend simply said her intuition told her that much synergy would result.*

That lady's name was Michelle Sera. Michelle and I connected on a call. I spent 60 minutes soaking up her energy and wisdom and jotting down notes like crazy. That day in February 2016 marked the beginning of a journey of self-discovery and deep inner learning toward *a future I could not even imagine before that introduction.*

If I had to pinpoint one very specific thing about my work with Michelle that has ultimately resulted in numerous quantum leaps in my life, it would be that action without alignment will surely not produce the result.

Michelle has helped me raise my level of awareness, get into alignment, and identify and conquer my limiting beliefs, resulting in one breakthrough after another.

Does it mean that every day is pure bliss? Well, to be honest, yes!

Why? Because I begin each day aware of where I am and where I want to go and aligned.

In the end, alignment is all that matters.

I know for a fact that this book contains the missing pieces for you to create your breakthrough.

Why do I know? Because this book is all about the foundational inner game that is the biggest and most important domino to reach your goals. Once the inner game is conquered, the outer has a knack for falling into place.

Turn the page, and start right now. I promise...you'll LOVE where it leads you.

Chris Spurvey

Chris Spurvey Sales Growth Consulting Inc.

Author: *It's Time to Sell - Cultivating the Sales Mind-Set*

Mt. Pearl, Newfoundland Canada

August 2022

INTRODUCTION

What you've always known, but never fessed up to...

Exercise: Set the stage for the results you want

> **Note:** There are tons of extras that come with this book, for free.
> To get yours, go to 7minuteshiftextras.com

The business you are building is actually not a business at all. It's an expression of your truest self. I think some part of you has always known this. It's an expression of your power to create, and everyone has that power; we are all creators. Just like the artist's sculpture, the Olympic athlete's medal-winning performance, or the actor's stage presence, your business is the evidence of your ability to create. It's a speck of the Zero-Point Field, God, the Universe, Quantum Field, Goddess, Source, or Higher Power (fill in the blank) in you. *This is vibrational.* It's a frequency.

The trouble with things that are an expression of self is that we riddle them with fear, doubt, and worry. And building a business of your own is a surefire way to trigger those negative feelings. Which is why I wrote this book, to give you the tools to eliminate those emotional stumbling blocks AND the awareness of your ability to create SO much more.

My goal for you is that you reach a place where you KNOW you and your business will succeed, and from this place of knowing, you manifest everything you desire.

Let me tell you something... you and every other person on this planet has access to the same frequencies. We all have the same amount of time in the day. We all have the same basic thoughts. It's how we manage these thoughts that enables one person to build a highly successful business with incredible results while another struggles to get client #1.

There is a solution, The 7-Minute Shift™ is how you will fix it.

If you find yourself thinking things like—Who am I to achieve such big things? Who am I to start a business, run a company, or lead? Who am I to call myself a coach? or, If I could succeed, I would have by now, or just plain…Who am I kidding!?—<u>then this little book is for you</u>.

I suggest you grab some supplies to dedicate to this book and the work we're going to do together. A notebook and pen is a good start. Or you can use this book. It's laid out as a workbook. Of course, if you prefer not to write in the book, you can download the companion guide (see below), and use that.

Here, in these pages, I'm going to share my biggest discovery—streamlined manifesting. After a few years of daily meditations, and too many methodologies to count, I decided there had to be a way to create the same results in minutes. There had to be something that I could do quickly, from anywhere, and over and over again to shift the results in my business.

About two years ago, I left my day job. I'd been working in marketing for a very long time. In the three years prior to leaving my job, I had coached over 900 people in marketing strategies to help them grow a business.

My experience while coaching was that a very small percentage of people would actually succeed. This is common knowledge in the online marketing education world, unfortunately. But I wanted to understand WHY. I observed more and listened intently. What I discovered was this:

It doesn't matter who you are, how much money you have, how much you invest in training, or how badly you need to succeed. If you have underlying negative beliefs about yourself, your chances of success, or even your ability to manage money, success, and attention, (all things a growing business brings), you will not get far.

And worse, you will only manifest more opportunities to back those negative beliefs. So you'll go around in circles, creating experiences to prove to yourself that you can't build a successful business, or you can't manage money well, or you aren't organized enough to pull it all together and make it work.

My realization that your state of mind has everything to do with reaching that knowing that you'll succeed, and the feeling of knowing is what enables you to manifest the people, opportunities, and resources to reach your goals is what ultimately led me down the path to here.

I've applied this awareness to my own businesses with incredible results. The 7-Minute Shift™ is the streamlined version of what I did to achieve results for myself and others.

I know you'll experience incredible results too.

I would like to say that I discovered The 7-Minute Shift overnight, that it came to me in a dream and was delivered in a matrix-y code-like message.

But it wasn't. Matter of fact, I came about this through life's ups and downs. Because I've had plenty of them. Any scars remind me of the contrast I experienced and how many times I gave up. And how many opportunities that contrast gave me to prove what I believe.

From the day that I was given a $1000 grant for women who had experienced trauma (more on this later), I decided I was finally going to build my own business, create loads of personal freedom, and enough financial overflow to never have to worry again.

Side Note: Doesn't matter how much money you have, some of us will still worry… A LOT. Unless we remove the perspective that created the belief that is fueling the worry.

But the business didn't happen simply because I made the decision. And it didn't happen quickly. I was missing a crucial piece of the manifesting puzzle. And because of this, I was repeating a pattern in my business attempts that felt terrible.

If you have a repeating pattern in relation to business, it's almost definitely an indicator that there's a limiting belief from an untrue perspective at work.

Every time I "failed," I felt betrayed and fooled. Embarrassed even. As if what I believed to be undeniable was a silly fantasy. Every single time I fell off the manifesting wagon, I'd limp away with bruised heart in hand, maybe even some shame.

There was a part of me that was certain that, as human beings, we are tapping into only a fraction of what we are, what we're capable of, and what we're here to do. Trouble was, I wasn't creating proof of it through consistent results. (Yet.) It hadn't really sunk in as to how much I WAS creating.

When I became aware that limiting beliefs and untrue perspectives were getting in the way of my ability to manifest, I finally began to experience consistency. I had to learn to bypass logic when it didn't serve me. I had to learn to elevate my mind to reality-shaping DEFCON 4, so I could shift the results in my business. But I hadn't yet made it a part of my daily practice because I didn't know how to let go of the perspectives that didn't serve me.

Actually, I had to learn how to (and you will to):

- Identify negative emotions being fueled by a belief
- Find the root perspective that created the belief
- Give my logical brain a reason to let it go

And as manifesting goes, I found a book, that led to a mentor (a few), that led to a process, that led to studying and mastering, which led to a certification.

I became certified as a Freedom Formula Facilitator and regularly use the Freedom Formula technique to free myself and countless others from the perspective that is getting in the way of a successful business. In addition, I am a Certified Happiness Coach, because well…it's what we're all after, right? *And it's a pretty awesome title too.*

All of this led to the creation of The 7-Minute Shift. Every step was manifesting in action. Every step was a breadcrumb on the trail to something much greater.

If you focus on elevating your state of mind first, then everything else will follow. Once I got this, everything shifted, incredible things happened, and I now have *several* successful businesses.

Your turn :)

As you cannonball into this book, here are a few suggestions:

1. Commit to mastering The 7-Minute Shift.
2. Complete the exercises.
3. Trust the process.
4. Love the process.
5. Send band-aids to the address listed at the end. (My sensitive self will need them after I have bared all.)

6. If you'd like to have the companion guide and other extras I created to go along with this book, they are free to you and can be downloaded at 7minuteshiftextras.com.

Here's a sneak peek into what you can expect:

Chapter 1: The First Thing You Need to Know (Chapter Name is a Secret)

Exercise: The Attraction Point Audit (Know the enemy of your success)

Chapter 2: The Second Thing You Need to Know (Chapter Name is a Secret)

Exercise: Awareness Sharpener (Eliminate what keeps you from certainty)

Chapter 3: Stop Spinning in Circles and Start Spinning Reality

Exercise: Make Me a Promise (This decision will move mountains in your business)

Chapter 4: Step 1: Why the Results You Want to See Are Delayed

Exercise: Detect Resistance (See the kink in the manifestation line)

Chapter 5: Step 2: The Sneaky Thing That is Holding Your Business Results Hostage

Exercise: Find the Vibrational Sinker

Chapter 6: Step 3: A Lightning-Fast Method for Creating Smooth Sailing to More Clients, Income, and Ease

Exercise: Let the Cork Float (Return to your innate manifesting abilities)

Chapter 7: Step 4: My Proven Hack for Fueling Manifestations in Your Business

Exercise: Borrowing Joy (Call up the key to manifesting results in a split second)

Chapter 8: Step 5: The Crazy Visual That Makes Your Brain Fall in Love With Your Goals

Exercise: The Eyes of You 2.0

Chapter 9: Step 6: Discover The Everyday Things That Can Raise Your Vibrational Frequency to Match Success

Exercise: Vibrational Increasers Hiding in Plain Sight

Chapter 10: Step 7: The Send Button for Your Business Results

Exercise: Hit the 'Send Button' for Your Business Manifestations

HOW TO USE THIS BOOK:

You have the opportunity to absorb every word in this book. Read it twice, if necessary, then apply immediately. This is important because if you are currently feeling any frustration, fear, doubt, worry, procrastination, uncertainty, not good enough-ness, or that maybe you're just not capable—you'll only create more opportunities to feel even more of these negative emotions.

That's why I created The 7-Minute Shift, so you'd have something to quickly shift your emotions and raise your vibration. Now you can work towards matching the frequency of wonderful results every single day.

You're going to learn how to elevate your mind, supercharge your entire body with emotions of joy and bliss, and incrementally increase your vibration till it becomes a match to the results you desire. It's not hard, it just takes practice.

Mantra Moment
Matching my state of mind and vibration creates the results I desire.

This book is me putting everything I know down on paper. Literally…everything I know and have experienced when it comes to manifesting and how I distilled it down to 7 minutes. Then applied it to business.

If I can get 1 million (heck, just 100) people to start using The 7-Minute Shift every single day to shift their business results, then the ripple effect will be astounding. It means you can create an amazing business that is a beautiful reflection and expression of you that touches every corner of the world in some way. It's almost better than brownies right out of the oven… almost.

But the real truth of why I'm giving this to you is because through the process, as we use your business as the focal point, something so un-fucking-believable will happen to you and your life. You will shift in ways you can't imagine at this point. You will attract things/people/and experiences that blow your mind. You will experience synchronicities. And you will change. Irrevocably. Beautifully.

So, it's time for the words of caution: If you don't want to know these things or experience breathtaking change, stop reading and put the book down. Give it to someone else. Because you can't unknow this once I spill it all. You can't go back.

Introduction Recap:

1. Your business is really an expression of your truest self.

2. How you feel, deep down, is a vibration that has a frequency.

3. That frequency is a match to something.

4. Fear, doubt, and worry will not grow your business.

5. You can reach a place where you KNOW you and your business will succeed.

6. This work will change you.

SECTION I
Preparing for The 7-Minute Shift

Still here?

Good.

By the end of this book, you will fully understand how to use The 7-Minute Shift, be using it, and shifting your results. You will have everything you need to manifest more clients, income, and ease, and more importantly, you will understand manifesting as a natural way of life. You may even begin to manifest really big things that blow the lid off your business.

But my truest, most secretive *don't-tell-a-soul* wish is this: That you'll realize in a split, mind-blowing second what's really been revealed to you and, as a result, know what you're capable of, relish it, roll around in it, and hold it close to your heart.

I'll guide you and help you however I can. This book will show you how to consciously manifest your path to becoming an abundant coach or business owner. You can create the business you dream of...promise.

I know this is only the "Introduction," but we have some exciting stuff to cover. Let's start the work.

You can go through this exercise here in the book or use the worksheets included in the bonus resources. You can download the bonus resources at 7minuteshiftextras.com.

Here's exercise #1: Set the stage for the results you want.

What do you want to manifest in your business?

_____

_____

_____

_____

_____

_____

_____

_____

_____

_____

_____

_____

_____

_____

_____

_____

What would it feel like to have those things? (List feelings for having each thing you've listed to manifest.)

_____

_____

_____

_____

_____

_____

_____

_____

_____

_____

_____

_____

_____

_____

_____

_____

_____

Do you believe you can manifest those things? (Be honest.)

_____

_____

_____

_____

_____

_____

_____

_____

_____

_____

_____

_____

_____

_____

_____

_____

_____

Do you believe you can HAVE these things? (Totally different from creating them, don't hold back).

_____

_____

_____

_____

_____

_____

_____

_____

_____

_____

_____

_____

_____

There are no right or wrong answers. Your answers will help us shape the work ahead and create bigger results, so don't sugar coat a thing.

I appreciate you.

"If you want to find the secrets of the universe, think in terms of energy, frequency and vibration."

— Nikola Tesla

CHAPTER 1
All Results Are Vibrational

Exercise: The Attraction Point Audit
(What are you currently attracting and why?)

I know, I know. This is an elusive concept. It's something we can kind of get intellectually when we think of things like sound, seismic activity, and even quantum elements. But to look around at your life and business and recognize that it all came about because of your vibration—well now, that's a little tough to hold on to.

The easiest thing for me is to remember that when we follow matter down to its smallest particle, then keep going, we end up in empty space—the space between those particles. That empty space is energy, and energy is vibration. Low, slow, high, fast, it's all a vibration. Everything is a vibration, and a vibration creates a frequency. And like two tuning forks set to the same frequency, activate one, and the other will also begin to vibrate, creating resonance. This is called sympathetic resonance, and it is a physically-observable scientific fact.

Kinda cool, right?

The thing about frequencies is we can't hear all of them, but would you really want to? I mean, imagine if every speck of matter in our reality had a frequency that was audible to human ears.

No wait... I don't want to imagine that.

It sounds like too much. I think my brain would explode. And THAT'S WHY we are limited to being able to hear only certain frequencies. Sanity is a good thing.

Back to the tuning fork concept. We need to create resonance with the frequency of the results we want. We begin to do this through our emotions or the way we feel.

Our emotions and the thoughts creating those emotions influence our vibration. So, we start here.

Mike Murphy, author of *The Creation Frequency* compares your vibrational frequency to that of an orchestra tuning up before a performance. He notes that your thoughts, emotions, and actions need to be attuned to one another to make beautiful music. Beautiful music is your successful business that your thoughts, emotions, and actions need to attune to.

Of course, as human beings, we run the gamut of emotions on any given day. If we look at our emotions from one second to the next, it would probably resemble the puppy who has the zoomies…running all over the place from one point to the next at full speed, till it drops from zoomies exhaustion.

Our emotions run all over the place too. *And sometimes we drop from exhaustion.*

But don't worry, you only need to look at your dominant positive emotions and your dominant negative emotions. It's essentially looking at averages. What a relief, right?!

I have a simple process for you to use to find your emotional average. In this exercise, you're going to identify a pattern that is your dominant negative emotion. This will shed some light on your current attraction point.

Your dominant negative emotion is a vibration, which in turn affects your vibrational baseline. This vibrational baseline creates a frequency that is a match to something. The Attraction Point Audit will uncover that something. *It's not as scary as it sounds, pinky swear.*

What you're currently attracting in your life and business and why is a crucial bit of awareness to have. Otherwise, how do we know where to go from here if we don't know where "here" is?

Ready?

I'm going to walk you through the Attraction Point Audit. I learned this process when I became certified as a Freedom Leader. This means that I am a Certified Freedom Formula Facilitator through the work of Nick Breau. He's a wonderful manifesting mentor who has made massive impacts in the world and in the lives of thousands of people, certainly mine.

Here goes:

Exercise: The Attraction Point Audit

(Know what's creating your current vibrational results.)

You can go through this exercise here in the book or use the worksheets included in the bonus resources. You can download the bonus resources at 7minuteshiftextras.com.

Answer the question for each area of your life below. It's important to answer what immediately comes up—don't overthink it. If nothing comes up, write down "none."

Surprise Bonus #1: I'll walk you through the Attraction Point Audit via video. Just go to 7minuteshiftextras.com to watch it, it's free.

What was/is the hardest thing about _____ and how did/does it make you feel?

1. Your business or your current employment or lack of employment

_____

_____

_____

_____

_____

_____

2. Previous employment (Last 1–3 jobs)

_____

_____

_____

_____

_____

_____

3. Your financial circumstances

_____

_____

_____

_____

_____

_____

4. Your current relationship or lack of relationship

_____

_____

_____

_____

_____

_____

5. Past relationships (Last 1–3 significant relationships)

_____

_____

_____

_____

_____

_____

_____

6. Family members (Is there anyone whom you have a struggle with?)

_____

_____

_____

_____

_____

_____

7. Past significant traumas

_____

_____

_____

_____

_____

_____

_____

8. Any other circumstance that comes up

_____

_____

_____

_____

_____

_____

Once you've taken the time to answer this question for 1–8, identify the pattern. What are the top 3 negative emotions across the board?

1. _____

2. _____

3. _____

These are the emotions that are likely the root causes behind any resistance, blocks, or limiting beliefs that are getting in the way of the results you'd like to see in your business. Having negative emotions contributes to your current vibration, and what resonates with that vibration is what you will attract in your business.

This is your current attraction point or vibrational baseline.

Mantra Moment

I can change my attraction point.

If you and I ever work together on this, we'll go a little deeper and may even cross-reference physical symptoms to most accurately identify your current attraction point. However, this is plenty to go on for now.

Look at your answers. Can you see a common pattern? Can you see one or two emotions showing up everywhere?

What do you think those emotions are creating in your vibrational reflection?

For example, never feeling good enough can be reflected back in your business as having no clients, clients who are unhappy, or clients who change their mind. Feeling any lack could manifest as money struggles, missed opportunities, and perceived repetitive failures.

Don't let this get to you. Only observe. I know how much you're worth, how SO good enough you are, and that any blocks are coming from perspectives you formed. These can be shifted. No matter who was involved in the creation of these perspectives, we can clear them away. I like to call this the CRUD Removal Service.

When we sign up for CRUD Removal Service, we Choose – Reframe – Untangle – Dissolve.

This is the deeper level of work I do with clients in my programs. It's really good stuff!

Chapter Recap:

1. All results are vibrational.

2. Your emotions and state of mind influence your vibration.

3. You have a current attraction point or vibrational baseline.

4. Sign up for CRUD Removal Service :)

Let's keep going.

"What is necessary to change a person is to change his awareness of himself."

—Abraham Maslow

CHAPTER 2

You are a _____ Earner

Exercise: Awareness Sharpener (Eliminate what keeps you from certainty.)

What if I said to you that all of your talent, expertise, education, skill, and hard work was not the reason for your results?

By results, I mean anything you've achieved. Your career, business, relationships, financial status, level of happiness and satisfaction in life, etc.

I can kind of guess how you might respond because I've seen the look on plenty of faces when I say this directly. Usually, one eyebrow rises slightly.

But remember that all results are vibrational, right?

Matter of fact, you are a vibrational earner. We are all vibrational earners. From day-to-day, we operate with goods, services, and paper or digital currency, but the real currency is vibration. You spend your endless supply of vibration, and in return, you get the vibrational match to your vibrational currency. You are a vibrational earner.

You earn what your vibration offers, hence we are vibrational earners. Earning by vibration precedes earning through your talent, expertise, education, skill, or hard work. Your vibration is what attracts the opportunity for those things to be needed, demanded, or given.

I learned the concept of being a vibrational earner from one of my mentors. This was one of many massive shifts in my awareness of self.

Let me share a story.

In addition to being a coach, I am a copywriter. I have been writing copy for entrepreneurs for over 15 years. Many of them make multi-millions. Some even more.

My copy has been the source of millions of dollars in revenue for my clients.

I do not have a college education. I am self-taught.

When I first started writing copy, I did so because I wanted to. I liked writing, and, being very sensitive to people's emotions, it seemed a good fit.

As I began to write for more and more people, my beliefs started getting in the way.

I'm not educated. I don't have a degree. I am not formally trained in copywriting.

Clients started dropping off.

When I started writing copy, I was following my highest excitement, having fun, listening to my inner guidance and all those wonderful nudges.

Until the perspective I formed when I dropped out of college kicked in.

I did not like college and struggled to stay focused. But I never really liked school to begin with. When I left college after only one semester, I felt like a failure. People had expected more of me. They expected great things, yada, yada, yada.

I made empty promises that I would go back. *As if that was the only way I could ever learn or succeed.*

I equated my inability to stay interested in four walls and mindlessly staring at an instructor as a lack of intelligence. And in turn, a lack in me, as in *not being good enough.*

For most of my adult life, I used intelligence as a wall between myself and others. I worked hard at what I call "intellectual shielding" because I didn't want to be stupid or disappoint those that had praised my intelligence as a child. I could kill two birds with one stone with intellectual shielding—prove I was smart and never become close to people that I'd later disappoint.

Rather than trusting that my true self was enough to create relationships or experiences with people, I put effort into making my intelligence evident. There was an underlying belief that no one would want/like/accept me otherwise. I had to show my value by showing how smart I was (or could come across as). I was not enough if not smart, quick, and "educated."

Have you ever felt like you had to come across as someone greater than you perceive yourself to be in order to be accepted and loved? It's an all too common thread among people. I can find something likeable in just about any human being on the planet but did not feel that others could find likable things about me. How sad. So, I shielded myself rather than feel the pain of any evidence that my beliefs about myself were true. I was so very fragile. And I believe that most human beings are... until they discover what they're truly capable of and can put away the shield.

In 2006, I was taking a taxi to the airport in Boston, Massachusetts. The driver struck up a conversation with me and eventually asked where I was from. I said, "Savannah, Georgia." He looked at me a little perplexed in his rearview mirror. Then said, "Huh, you don't have an accent; you actually sound half intelligent."

My deep belief that my value lies in my level of education was reflected to me. I'm not saying that my value IS in my level of education—clearly, it's not. But back then, I believed it was. My vibration was tuned into the frequency of low self-esteem, education equals value, lack of education equals no value, and that my decisions and choices always disappointed others. I also believed that being from the South was a bad thing. I believed that people would perceive me as less intelligent because of growing up at the end of a dirt road in the middle of Nowhere, Georgia. It was all MY perceptions, never anyone else's.

Ludicrous really. But there you have it. So, the comment from the taxi driver was spot on—a direct reflection of my vibrational frequency. As long as I continued to believe that of myself, I would attract experiences to feel it and in turn bolster the perspective. And that's how the cycle continues.

The taxi driver was not at fault. No one was. It was vibrational and in my ability to shift. But I did not understand that back then, and needless to say, the remainder of the trip was rather quiet.

Can you see the reflection I was creating in my world?

Little did I know, my education, my choices, or where I was from had nothing to do with my results (in life, work, and business), but I would certainly learn so.

My success as a copywriter could have ended that moment when self-doubt kicked in.

But, while I didn't know what I know now, I knew enough to keep following my heart and, in doing so, raised my vibration around copywriting higher and higher and higher.

And the results showed it. Within one year, I had a handful of steady clients. I continued to write copy as a side gig for many years (It took me a while to gain confidence and clear away the self-doubt, worry, and fear). It was this side gig that I had built and taught myself to do that ultimately enabled me to walk away from the full-time job that was crushing me. Today, I have even more steady clients and usually have a waitlist about three times a year.

My copywriting business will go over six figures with only being full-time for about two years. AND with the exception of a few conversations in fb groups when I started this over 15 years ago, I've never done one ounce of marketing to get copywriting clients. It has all been referrals—they just continue to show up. I attribute that flow and abundance to following my highest excitement and clearing the way of beliefs, perspectives, and negative emotions. I manifested it all. I created these results by working on the vibrational level of me and what I believed was possible.

All results form from instructions sent via a frequency (your emotions, thoughts, feelings) and while your talent, expertise, education, skill, and hard work contributes to your vibrational baseline which then determines your results, it isn't the cause of your results. You bring your desires, preferences, or goals into your life by matching your vibration (via thought and emotion) to the high vibration of those desired outcomes.

Your vibration is the means by which you are a vibrational earner.

I'll let that soak in a minute. *I had to sit with this one for a while myself.*

When we assume we understand the cause of something without following the tracks back to the true source, we struggle to create or avoid that something again.

Every action, choice, thought, or belief begins with the energy you bring to it. Your talent, expertise, education, skill, and even hard work are influenced by the energy you bring, by your state of mind. And that is the vibrational precursor.

Mantra Moment

I am a vibrational earner.

If you work hard because you believe that's necessary, you will likely get some results, yes, but it's generally fleeting or it doesn't last, and you feel like you're chasing results instead of attracting. You're expelling much more energy and effort than necessary when you should be broadcasting high vibrations to attract effortlessly.

Have you ever had the experience of working really really hard to achieve something and you did it only to lose all the momentum and results months later (or worse, end up with nothing to show for it)?

You didn't have the vibrational foundation to hold it.

There's a difference between working really hard because it's what you believe you must do vs. feeling inspired to work really hard. They create very different outcomes.

The belief that you must work hard to achieve results or that you must work hard to be worthy of results has its own vibrational frequency. And it is a very different vibrational frequency from the belief that all results are vibrational. They feel different, right? Try reading the lines below and compare how they feel:

I must work really hard to have what I want.

I must work really hard to be worthy of what I want.

I must work really hard to deserve these things.

I must work really hard to deserve success.

I am worthy because I was born worthy.

I am a vibrational earner.

I deserve to have what I want.

I am already successful.

If you, instead, remember that you are a vibrational earner, then that changes things. What you earn and achieve is based on how well your vibration matches those things. AND how consistently you hold your higher vibration and how you manage your state of mind from day-to-day.

Which leads me to my next point: Bringing your awareness to your vibrational percentages.

This work came from an incredible mentor of mine—Kent Petersen. He taught me to cultivate a level of awareness I had not previously had. By tracking vibrational percentages, I gained more influence over my vibrational field. From this level of awareness, I gained a much clearer picture of where I really was on a day-to-day basis vibrationally. And what I was earning from it.

This kind of awareness enables you to manifest more of the results you want, more consistently. (I bet you didn't think that was possible! It is, and you will.)

There are three stages to shifting the results in your business through the foundation of your vibrational baseline.

1. Awareness

2. Alignment

3. Action

Never, ever, ever try to take action without first bringing your awareness into focus and making sure you are in alignment.

Acting *without awareness* and *out of alignment* is just reacting. It doesn't get you far.

Right now, we're working on bringing your awareness into focus. This way, you know where you're starting, know the real picture, and can shift in the appropriate direction that actually gets you results (like more clients, income, and ease). You cannot reach a deep knowing that your business will succeed without first having awareness of how you feel about it and what you believe is possible.

Through these pages, you're going to learn how to focus your awareness, so you can quickly address anything getting in the way of the results you want to see.

You are a vibrational earner. That's it. Nothing else you have or do is relevant at this point.

I only want to talk to you and your vibration right now. *I will let other versions of you into the room later.*

As you continue to read this book, you will understand awareness, alignment, and action intimately. By the time you are done, you will know that if you ever get stuck or feel discouraged, you just come back to them. They are your homebase.

Here's your next exercise:

Exercise: The Awareness Sharpener (Eliminate what keeps you from certainty.)

You can go through this exercise here in the book or use the worksheets included in the bonus resources. You can download the bonus resources at 7minuteshiftextras.com.

Draw a pie chart every day for the next seven days. At the end of each day, I want you to fill in that pie chart with how much of the day your thoughts around your business were positive.

Most people are surprised when they actually bring their attention to this. It's usually much lower than they realize.

As my mentor, Kent, pointed out, if your day was 50% positive, that means that 50% of your vibration today was elevated. But that also means that half of the day it was not elevated, so there's a lot of room for improvement.

Track your vibrational percentages over the next 7 days and become more aware.

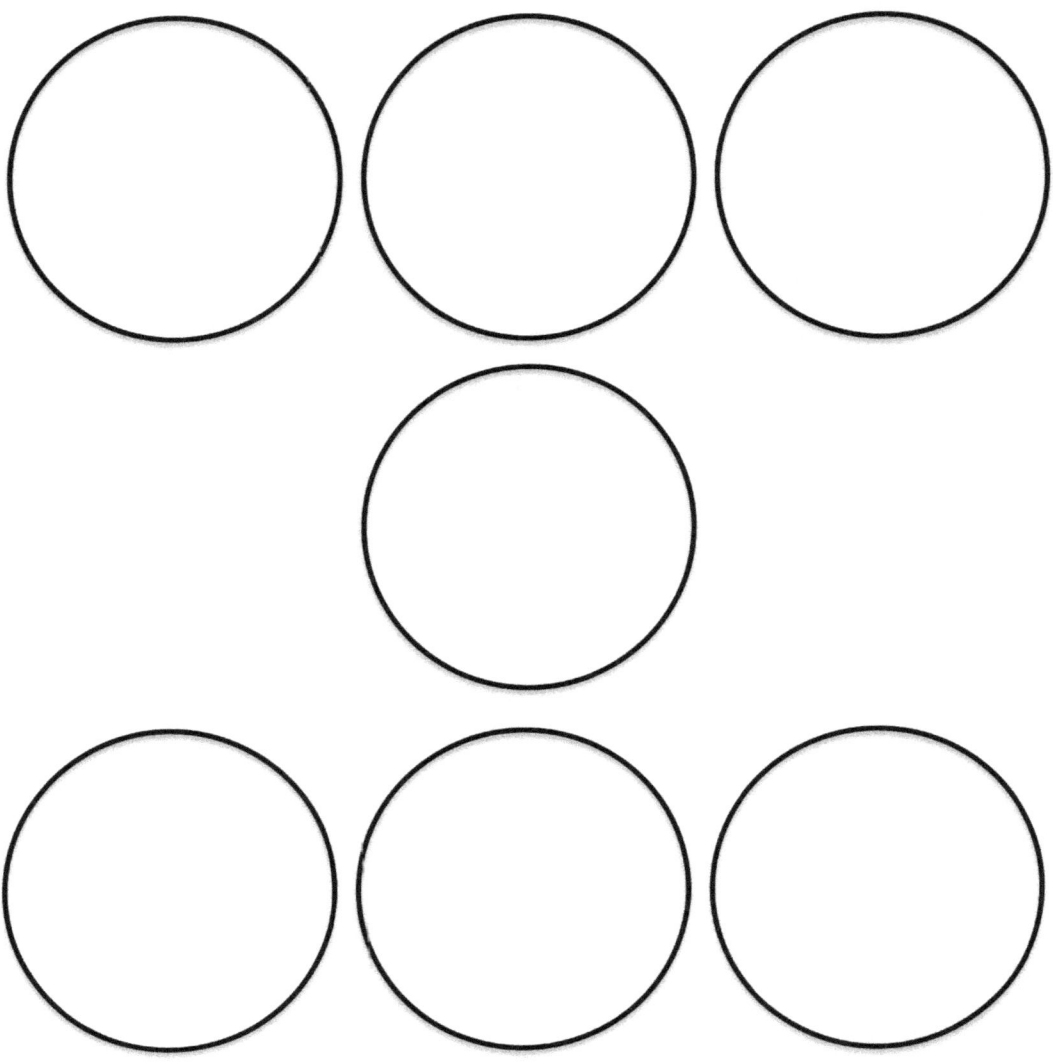

Chapter Recap:

1. You are a vibrational earner.

2. Hard work from a place of misalignment does not create what you desire.

3. Sharpening your awareness enables you to fine-tune your vibration.

4. Track your vibrational percentages.

"What we achieve inwardly will change outer reality."

—Plutarch

CHAPTER 3

Stop Spinning in Circles and Start Spinning Reality

Exercise: Make Me a Promise
(This decision will move mountains in your business.)

In August of 2015, I hit my lowest point. I was going through a divorce after 23 years of marriage (my whole adult life basically). I was starting over at 40ish and had two teenagers at home. I was working a job that was long hours, standing all day with copy machines, churning out stacks of print projects, with barely enough time for one bathroom break a shift.

So of course, I didn't drink water. I ended up in the ER with kidney pain and a fever. I didn't have insurance.

Oh—and I was being stalked. My life had been threatened. And I lived in the downtown district of a small city across from a rowdy bar that held karaoke a few times a week that ran until 2 a.m. *I could sing along with everyone from my bed.* Cool, right?

I was exhausted, stressed out, terrified, and mentally on my last pinch of "strength." This had not ever been my life, nor was it the life I wanted, but I didn't know how to get out of it.

On one particular night, I awoke with my heart pounding out of my chest. It was around 3 a.m., I sat up and put my feet on the cold floor waiting to hear it again. I'd heard the crunch of heavy bootsteps up the gravel driveway right outside of my window.

That gravel driveway led to my porch and front door. Well, it was a door that came into my kitchen. There was a heavy screen door with iron bars, then the wooden door that led into the kitchen. My room was off the kitchen. My kids' rooms were in the back of the house.

Some nights I heard the screen door with iron bars creak open. Some nights I heard the wooden door of the kitchen open. Some nights I heard footsteps in the kitchen. Every night I heard something. Every night it was the same—I'd be woken from a dead sleep, heart pounding because I heard someone coming in. I'd jump up and check the house because I couldn't take the chance that it was real and let someone get to my kids.

But every night it was not real. My mind was creating auditory hallucinations because my stress levels were too high. This went on for about two months.

Finally, tired and teary, I came home from work one night, sat down on the sofa and just cried till there was nothing left. I couldn't go on like this. I didn't want to. I decided to close my eyes and pretend that everything was ok. Better than ok, amazing. I would spend all the time I could daydreaming about my fairytale farm in a little mountain valley where it was peaceful, safe, and beautiful.

I escaped as often as I could because it was the only thing that made everything tolerable. *Slowly but surely, things began to change.*

A woman walked into the print services department I managed to have a brochure created and printed. She was from a women's non-profit that awarded grants to women who had experienced hard times, trauma, or abuse. She was very kind and was appreciative of the help I gave her. As she was leaving, she paused and looked back at me.

"I don't know why it's so hard to give this money away. We have so much to give and can't find a single woman to give it to." I swear she had a sparkle in her eye as she said it.

I looked at the brochure and saw that the requirement was to write your story. So, I wrote mine and submitted it.

I was awarded a $1000 grant and was invited to speak to the local group for this organization.

Three months later, they reached out and said, "We have an extra $1200 left over and we'd like to give it to you."

Seriously.

Soon after, a friend told me about a marketing job that she thought I'd be a good fit for. I applied, interviewed, and was hired. Within two weeks, I went from standing all day making copies to my own office creating marketing materials for a casino.

I was astonished that all of this was happening. But I was 100% convinced that it was tied to my daydreaming. Even though I knew about "manifesting," the analytical side of me needed something more concrete to understand HOW it was happening.

Be careful what you ask for. You just might get it.

It all started with a desire for something better.

You have a desire. A desire to grow a business that is filled with work you love to do that generates more than enough financial wealth and abundance to give you personal freedom, a sense of security, expansion, and flexibility to choose what you do with your days.

You want to make an impact, which is to say, be needed in a way that completes the whole. My interpretation of this is that you need to remember what it's like to BE whole, to remember you are THE whole, life, existence, and the very essence of creation.

But I digress. Let's get back on track.

If you want to be free to work half a day on Monday, then Tuesday–Thursday, then take Friday–Sunday off to play outside of your business, never, for one second worrying about whether there's enough money this month or clients coming in next week, *you're on the right track.*

If you'd like to silence the doubt that swims around in your head or cyclically presents itself when you least need it, *you're in the right place.*

And finally, if you'd like to breeze past fear rather than tumble into the thoughts that have you terrified of failing, going broke, disappointing others, and losing things (and people) who matter to you… *you're ready to learn what I'm about to share.*

I was in all of these states of mind for a long time, and not only was it stressful, but it also hammered my well-being over and over again till I didn't know which way was up. It crushed my sense of self and drowned my ambition. Till I said, "That's it, no more."

Mantra Moment

This is my personal favorite:

I am healthy, wealthy, strong and vibrant.

Having manifested many things in my life, I took note. I looked for evidence that struggle isn't necessary. I studied. Then I made the biggest commitment of my life: that I would grow a business from the inside out and focus on my one and only job…to maintain my state of mind. I had a sneaking suspicion that if I elevated my state of mind, everything else would follow.

That's exactly what I did.

Now, I'm showing you step-by-step, the daily practice I use to manifest more clients, income, and ease. Learning this stuff changes how you make decisions, take action in your business, and see the future. Starting immediately, I want you to use it to eliminate doubt and worry and shrug off fear. Ever see a duck flap its wings and shake things off? How about your dog (no wings, just shaking it off)? That's what I'm talking about.

The 7-Minute Shift addresses it all:

- Doubts, fears, and worries
- Your state of mind
- Changing the way you see yourself
- How you make decisions
- Raising your vibrational frequency
- And making it all stick

In 7 minutes or less a day.

It will take a little practice, but it's worth it. When I began applying this every single day, I actually created a waiting list of clients in one of my businesses! Literally, a waiting list! Abso-lute-ly amazing.

Here are four things my mentors taught me that are really relevant here…

- Success is a feeling, not a thing.
- No one can give you anything. You can only be given what you give yourself. (Because what you receive is a reflection, get it?)
- Your world is a mirror. You have to smile first to see it come back to you. You have to give yourself the feeling of success for success to come back to you.
- If you give yourself feelings of far worse things, those far worse things will find you. Trust me here, I've lived it.

Here's the thing… you are creation manifested. Literally. You are creation in physical form. Creation manifested itself. (You, in your highest vibratory form—light—consciousness—manifested your physical form.)

So of course, you can manifest!

You ARE something that manifests. 24/7. You can't turn it off because you are IT. You are manifesting, manifestation, and potential unfolding. You are reality's conductor. To put it plainly: *You cannot NOT manifest.*

So, you're left with two choices:

1. Continue to manifest unconsciously, succumb to fear, doubt, and worry, repetitive "failures" and trudge through what life throws at you, or…

2. Become aware and consciously manifest, shape your business reality into everything you want it to be.

If you choose #1, I can tell you it won't be easy. You'll experience ups and downs, frustration and exhaustion, and question who you are and what you're capable of.

If you choose #2, the sky's the limit. You'll still experience ups and downs, but you'll have a clear understanding of how to shift your energy, emotions, and vibration rather than succumbing to it. You'll expose the true nature of life, creative expression, and the potential hidden under the guise of your business. You'll manifest TONS.

No, Morpheus, we do not need to choose the red or blue pill. *That sounds sketchy.* How about we just use The 7-Minute Shift instead.

My Disclaimer: It's true that many succeed with outer action only, while some just spin in circles no matter how hard they try. It's these people (you and me) who must approach with inner action. Circle spinners never give up, are passionate about the journey, and are incredibly self-aware. *Eventually, we spin reality and create long-lasting results.*

You will shift the results in your business.

Before we move on to the actual steps of The 7-Minute Shift, I want you to know that...

I appreciate you.

Exercise: Make Me a Promise (This decision will move mountains in your business.)

You can go through this exercise here in the book or use the worksheets included in the bonus resources. You can download the bonus resources at 7minuteshiftextras.com.

Write the following sentence:

Michelle, fellow creator of worlds, I promise I will create the results in my business that I want to see. I will follow each and every step you teach, trust the process, and above all, consciously direct what I manifest. Starting right now, right this second, I will never unconsciously manifest again and instead, embrace inner work as a lifestyle. I am a creator of worlds too, so my only job is to elevate my state of mind and shift my results. *Easy peasy.*

_____

_____

_____

_____

_____

_____

_____

Chapter Recap:

1. You cannot not manifest. You manifest 24/7 by default, so consciously manifest.

2. Elevate your state of mind…everything else follows.

3. You are a creator of worlds.

4. The 7-Minute Shift is the way forward.

SECTION II
The 7-Minute Shift™

"Most of us have two lives: the life we live, and the unlived life within us. Between the two stands Resistance."

—Steven Pressfield

CHAPTER 4
The 7-Minute Shift

Step 1: Why The Results You Want To See Are Delayed
Exercise: Detect Resistance (See the kink in the manifestation line.)

Remember when I mentioned the three phases of manifesting? AWARENESS, ALIGNMENT, and ACTION? This is important to remember for a couple of reasons:

1. You will shift through ALL of these three phases in The 7-Minute Shift. (You'll do this daily.)

2. If you ever find yourself stuck, come back to the first phase(awareness) of the three phases.

That might look like this:

Sharpen your *AWARENESS*. Where are you at? What are you feeling? What doesn't feel right?

Get into *ALIGNMENT*. This can be as simple as taking a deep breath. *Really.* I mean, you can also call up a memory of a time that made you feel incredible happiness and joy. *But in a pinch, just breathe.*

And then, and only then, *ACTION*. What feels good to do? What do you want to do? What would you prefer to do? And so on.

Think of this as triage. You always have The 7-Minute Shift, but if you can't do that, just go back to awareness, alignment, and then, and only then—action. Then proceed.

I want to emphasize how important it is that you begin to use these three steps all the time. They are meant as a structure to follow to help you master self and manage your state of mind easily.

Starting with the awareness phase, you are going to become aware of any negative emotions, especially those around your business. You are going to detect resistance.

Let's say, you're starting your day and you are doing your 7-Minute Shift. Step 1: Detect Resistance.

You want to find what's responsible for a lower vibration or low frequency. What's creating resistance to a higher vibration (if anything)?

As one of my mentors told me, "The cork always floats." We are the cork. But over time, sinkers get added to the line, and with enough sinkers, the cork can begin to get pulled under. If you remove the sinkers, the cork goes back to floating, high vibing, and bringing you into an elevated state of mind.

So, you ask yourself, "How am I feeling towards my business?" or even just, "How am I feeling?"

> **STOP:** It's really important to stop right here and let you know to NOT overthink any of this. Your subconscious will tell you the answers you need, and more importantly, the right answers. No matter how silly, illogical, or just nonsensical the answers are, go with them.

If you have any dominant negative emotions around your business, they will pop up. If you have a feeling of dread or frustration, you'll become aware of it immediately.

You may not even have to ask yourself how you're feeling, you may already know.

Now, you may not have any negative feelings coming up, that's okay, you're going to shift to step #4 if that's the case. (More explanation at step 4)

Recap: Ask yourself if there are any negative emotions weighing on you today? Especially in relation to your business. Are you feeling discouraged? Or worn out? Identify the negative emotion.

Example: I am feeling frustrated about money today. Clients aren't paying me on time.

Or I'm feeling discouraged, like none of this is working. Or I NEED clients to start showing up! Or maybe, I'm tired, I don't want to touch my laptop, I don't want to write another email.

Just bring your awareness to the feeling. This feeling, if left alone and undetected, will influence your thoughts throughout the day. Those negative thoughts lower your vibration.

Hold up. Another I-have-to-tell-you moment: If you have a bad day, you have not destroyed your vibration. You have not set off a series of catastrophic events and mistakenly manifested terrible things. If you hold a negative emotion long enough, it can become a dominant negative emotion and that will begin to influence your reality. *But it takes more than a day.*

And you can turn it around to a positive emotion rather quickly. That is what the 7-Minute Shift is designed to do (along with a few other things).

Which brings me to another important point. First, let me ask you a question. If you wanted to feel really bad, down in the dumps, you could probably access that low vibe pretty easily, right? I mean, I, for one, can call up a plethora of memories and imagined futures that will drag me to the bottom of the ocean faster than a two-ton boulder.

But do I want that? NO. Just as you can easily access the low state of mind, you can access the elevated state of mind. It's no different. If you can access the low easily, you can access the high easily.

It's just a choice. And something to practice.

That statement used to make me really, really angry. When you struggle with a low state of mind all the time, it really feels like a slap in the face to be told it's a choice, *but hear me out.*

We're going to talk about a new version of you shortly, but for now, let me just say that you can choose to feel more of what you prefer. This other version of you doesn't feel the same as this version of you, so you can choose to feel differently.

You can choose to not react to things that typically make you feel low (Even though the "old" you might.)

You can choose to see your current circumstances as results from your past thoughts, emotions, and perspectives and that this is currently in a state of change. The negative circumstances are on their way out the door because you are changing your thinking and, therefore, your vibrational frequency.

You can choose to acknowledge that there are likely several interpretations of the events that formed your beliefs (that created negative feelings) that *could* mean your interpretation is not true.

You can use these moments as opportunities to dig down into the new version of you even further.

You can make it a game. (And no, I'm not trying to talk to you like a six-year-old who needs to clean their room, more like a highly competitive athlete.)

Pretend you're on a football field… *Wait, Michelle, I will never be on a football field.* Ok, how about anything you have done competitively?

I used to race dragon boats, so I can imagine that I am on the ocean in a dragon boat, and I'm about to race another dragon boat. The gun goes off, and I'm paddling. There are some obstacles up ahead, but I'm determined to win this race, so I show off how good I am at paddling this two-ton boat. I am incredibly strong and trust myself to pull the water with my oar and make this boat move.

Show off how competitive you can be and win this race. Every circumstance that arises (as you shift) is your opportunity to laugh it off and say, "I will win! THIS is how I react now. This is how strongly I believe that I create my reality."

When you decide you want something, you don't give up easily. You want this new version of you and this new reality and this new version of your business, so choose it. Use every moment you can to prove who you are now and to prove how much you influence your reality.

Okay, enough of my rant.

As I go through the actual steps of The 7-Minute Shift, each step is the exercise for the chapter. Since you are learning The 7-Minute Shift, I recommend that you write these exercises down (or use the downloadable guide).

You'd be shocked at how many people struggle with step 1 of The 7-Minute Shift.

As human beings, we avoid addressing negative feelings. While we may entertain them, rant through them, and commiserate with others about them, we rarely call them out and release them. Manifesting big shifts doesn't happen when negative emotions are bogging down communications, creating traffic jams, or attracting more negative vibrations. Aka, pulling the cork under.

Remember, like attracts like. You are essentially learning to clean the slate and move forward. As you do this each day, you move forward from a higher state of mind or vibrational frequency. And THAT creates the magic!

Mantra Moment

My natural state is to create.

As you begin to practice this daily, you'll get faster and faster. I don't write anything down anymore, I do all of this in my head (except for the action steps) or I say them out loud—as long as doing so won't make anyone around concerned for their safety, lol.

Exercise: Detect Resistance (See the kink in the manifestation line.)

You can go through this exercise here in the book or use the worksheets included in the bonus resources. You can download the bonus resources at 7minuteshiftextras.com.

Write down how you're feeling. Identify any negative feelings around your business. If you have negative feelings around something outside of your business, go ahead and write that down because it will affect everything anyway.

Example of the negative feeling identified, or resistance detected: I am frustrated about money, clients aren't paying on time, and I need it.

Please don't sugar coat this. Don't gloss over it. Even if it sounds really childish, write it down. It's an important clue that we're going to need in the next step.

_____

_____

_____

_____

_____

PS: I thought I'd give you a tip on what to do if you have a bad day. Of course, you're always going to do The 7-Minute Shift, but here's a little extra:

We all have days that aren't the greatest. Our moods fall off the cliff and all you want to do is veg out and watch Netflix.

Or read another sci fi/fantasy trilogy—okay, maybe that's me. But the point is, you're human.

When you begin doing THIS work—focusing on managing your state of mind to raise your vibration and shift results in your business, you can get really hooked on the great days. And that is the point really, keeping your vibration high to resonate with your desires.

When you are experiencing that super high bliss (and it will happen), it can feel like nothing is impossible.

Part of maintaining a high vibration is knowing how to intentionally act (not react) when we hit a bump in the road. Here are some common bumps you may experience.

A family member calls with a bit of bad news or just ranting about something that you don't prefer to be subjected to.

A client falls through.

You feel a little overwhelmed by your current workload.

Your car is having brake issues AGAIN.

Or you watched a little too much YouTube over the weekend.

I've experienced all of these things, and I'm here to tell you it's okay. It's not going to crash your vibration; trust me, it's nothing like the stock market or the fickleness of crypto.

Now, here's what you do:

1. Bring your attention back to your **awareness**—how much of your day is filled with negative thoughts? Neutral thoughts are just fine. But you need to be aware of how much is actually negative.

2. Next, get into **alignment**. This means do something that makes you feel better. Take a walk, go read your favorite book, listen to some music, talk with a friend. Rest,

Michelle Sera

relax. Call up a memory of a time you felt the way you'd really like to feel right now (*works every time*).

3. Action—only inspired **action**. What do you want to do? What feels really good to do right now? Even if it's pulling out that art project you've been wanting to do or jumping on your mountain bike for a couple of hours—go do it.

> **Surprise Bonus #2:** Go get your happiness toolkit. Go to 7minuteshiftextras.com, it's free.

The cool thing that happens when you follow these steps, even if you only take that inspired action for 5–10 minutes, it shifts your state of mind.

Here's the part I know you really want to hear:

Your vibration is set through your dominant emotions. If you have a bad day, but shift out of it, your good days far outnumber your bad days.

The more you do the work, the more it becomes a way of life, and the higher your vibrational baseline becomes. You will be more resilient, so even when your mood dips, you don't dip as far as you used to, and it does NOT lower your vibration.

Does that make sense?

That's why it's so important to start the work—just get started and commit to it every single day NOW. (It's momentum-based)

You are <u>what</u> determines the reality you experience. Got that? It is your innate ability to influence reality and make it your own.

Chapter Recap:

1. There are three phases to manifesting: AWARENESS, ALIGNMENT, and ACTION.

2. These three phases are also your triage.

3. Negative feelings will influence your thoughts, lowering your vibration

4. How good can you get at reacting differently? Dragon Boats rule, football fields drool (Have you ever heard, 'Boys drool, girls rule? No? Guess I'm dating myself again)

59

"It's useful to go out of this world and see it from the perspective of another one."

—Terry Pratchett

CHAPTER 5

The 7-Minute Shift

Step 2: The Sneaky Thing That is Holding Your Business Results Hostage
Exercise: Find the Vibrational Sinker

All throughout life, we form perspectives. Everything we experience, in turn, causes us to create a perspective. A perspective isn't good or bad, it is just a means of measuring, observing, and interpreting the physical world and our interactions with it.

The thing about forming a perspective is that we determine reality with it. We close down all potential into one possibility with one meaning. Our perspectives form beliefs which open doors and close doors. Beliefs form the invisible walls of our reality and can make our experience of our reality limited. Beliefs also fuel emotions (and vice versa).

Here's an example of how this perspective thing might happen and show up:

Many people form a negative perspective about "wealthy" people. Matter of fact, while I was putting together a presentation for a virtual summit recently, I needed an image of a "wealthy" person. When I searched those terms, in the top three results was an image of a man in a suit, with a cigar in one hand, a drink in the other, and a young, attractive woman on each side of him. Worse, he had a condescending smirk on his face.

THAT is a perception of what a "wealthy" person might be like. If you are building a business and have a similar perception, you may unconsciously resist becoming wealthy because you don't want to become what you believe a wealthy person is.

Similarly, if you've ever purchased a high-ticket program, you likely had a phone conversation with a sales person. While most of these calls are genuinely interested in finding a fit between the buyer and the program offered, some are not so selective. They need the sale no matter what, so they resort to highly manipulative tactics. If you've ever experienced this, you may form the idea that sales are bad or people who try to sell are not good people with integrity.

Neither of these scenarios is true, but both are very common negative perspectives getting in the way of success. I hear it all the time.

These are also considered limiting beliefs.

Additional clues that limiting beliefs are at play show up as:

Being uncomfortable with charging more.

Having difficulty sharing or showing up on social media.

Not believing you can manage a business.

Not believing that you have enough knowledge, expertise, or experience to help others.

Resisting growing your business even bigger.

The emotions that are wrapped up in these limiting beliefs can be triggered in your day-to-day business activities such as…

You want to spend money on marketing – triggered.

You want to join a mastermind – triggered.

You want to sell your program – triggered.

You want to grow your business, but don't trust yourself – triggered.

The problem starts when a negative perspective is formed, then it can branch off of itself and form more negative perspectives, which then turn into negative beliefs, and finally, opportunities for these negative emotions to affect the results in your business.

And on and on it goes, one roadblock after another, keeping you from the results you want. Worse, you may possibly form a perspective that manifesting doesn't work.

HA! That is the equivalent of saying YOU don't work. Or standing in the middle of a stream and saying the water doesn't work. *It just doesn't make sense.*

And when we can give your subconscious mind evidence that your current negative perspective doesn't serve you, then we can help your subconscious see that it doesn't make sense to hold onto that perspective anymore. Then it's gone. *Just like that, you can let it go.*

So, what is the specific perspective, or perspectives, holding you back?

A simple statement or question can help find it.

Exercise: Find the Vibrational Sinker/s

You can go through this exercise here in the book or use the worksheets included in the bonus resources. You can download the bonus resources at 7minuteshiftextras.com.

The process I just walked you through is your exercise for this chapter. Practice it. You can probably find a few perspectives that need shifting right now. These perspectives that don't serve you, think of them as sinkers.

Remember, the quote I shared from one of my mentors, "The cork always floats."

You are the cork. You are naturally and innately happy. But as you move through life and have experiences from which you form perspectives and beliefs that create negative emotions and feelings, sinkers get added to the line. *And the cork eventually gets pulled under.*

If you can remove the sinker or sinkers on a daily basis—you'll find that you float. You float in bliss and joy and happiness. You float in a sea of potentiality. Anything is possible. Everything is possible. And just like that, you begin to shift your business results without needing another piece of marketing, another offer, another ad campaign, etc.

Mantra Moment

The cork always floats. I am the cork.

Those things can come later when you're floating and making decisions from a really high vibrational frequency AND those decisions feel right.

Creates a totally different outcome!

To put step 2: Finding the Vibrational Sinker (aka Perspective) into action, let's do the next exercise. Start by asking yourself this question:

What do I believe is true about myself that's causing [fill in the blank]?

_____

_____

_____

_____

_____

_____

_____

_____

_____

Another way to uncover perspectives is to complete this statement:

I am [insert negative circumstance] because I...

_____

_____

_____

_____

_____

_____

_____

_____

_____

_____

Example 1:

What do I believe is true about myself that's causing clients to not pay me on time?

It's because my work is not good enough.

Example 2:

I am feeling frustrated over clients not paying me because I clearly am not doing good enough work.

The perspective that's not serving you: Clients aren't paying me on time because I'm not doing good enough work. The core perspective is "I'm not good enough."

You may have to try rewording your statement a few times to hit upon the vibrational sinker. You'll feel it when the words are right because it will magnify the negative feeling you are having. Write down whatever answer pops into your mind. Do NOT overthink the question. It doesn't have to be logical or make sense, we're digging out the roadblocks and that's usually, to some degree, nonsensical.

More Examples:

I believe that I'm failing at something in order to be experiencing clients not paying me on time.

I believe my clients aren't happy, so they're not paying me.

I believe this was too good to be true, so of course it's falling apart now, and the money's not coming in.

I believe that these clients changed their mind (another version of too good to be true).

Extra Credit Work: Take this a step further and ask yourself:

What do I believe that could account for this perspective?

_____

_____

_____

_____

_____

_____

_____

_____

_____

_____

_____

_____

_____

_____

Go quickly, till you land on something that feels simple and on the mark. Don't spend too long on this step. As you practice this daily, you will get very fast at figuring this out. And it's okay if every now and then you don't get to an answer that is spot on, just close. Proceed with the steps of The 7-Minute Shift anyway and make a note to revisit this later. Journal on it, talk it through out loud, whatever it takes to untangle it and see it for what it is.

And let me just say... you are amazing. No, I don't know you personally (not yet), and I don't know who you are. If you're here, reading this and giving it a shot, then I know you're brave. I know you're insightful and self-aware. I know you want to achieve things and believe you are capable of so much more.

I know you have integrity, and people matter to you. I know you are willing to do what it takes. *All results are vibrational, don't forget it.*

I am in appreciation of you and your willingness to explore. How great will it be when more of us are consciously manifesting and creating a higher vibrational frequency to bring others into resonance and synchronicity?

Pretty darn great.

Much love.

Chapter Recap:

1. Repeating patterns are an indicator of a limiting belief at work.

2. You have to learn to bypass logic when it doesn't serve you.

3. Perspectives can be changed and beliefs that aren't helpful can be let go.

4. **Secret tip:** Be happy with what you have AND want more.

"I've learned that being whole is the perfect state of creation. I've seen this time and time again in witnessing true healings in people all over the world."

—Joe Dispenza

CHAPTER 6
The 7-Minute Shift

Step 3: A Lightning-Fast Method for Creating Smooth Sailing to More Clients, Income, and Ease
Exercise: Let the Cork Float (Return to your innate manifesting abilities.)

I want to pause for a moment and breathe. *Take a deep breath with me.* This is an excellent way to come to the present moment and remember that there's nothing else. It's a fast and easy way to get into alignment.

You're learning a lot with each step of The 7-Minute Shift. The great thing about going through it in this book and doing the steps as exercises is that soon, you'll be able to breeze through this in 7 minutes or less (I think it takes me only 4 or 5 minutes some days) and in doing so, create BIG changes.

You'll begin to shift the results in your business for sure. It happens in a myriad of ways. It can be as simple as an idea popping into your mind out of nowhere. Or meeting someone who then connects you with someone else, etc. Or a new client being referred to you or multiple clients showing up at once. (It's always strange to me how they seem to come in clusters.) Or simply more money showing up, more income streams, and well…just MORE.

That's nature. AND the nature of the Universe. It expands, grows, creates stuff, and just keeps going. When we, as human beings, tap into that ability within ourselves, we become so much more aligned with Universal Laws and everything really.

When we, as the human race, tap into this more collectively, geez…who knows what will happen.

For now, though, I want you to just breathe as we move into reframing. Reframing is a common practice in many mindset modalities. It's perfect here because we can use it to quickly release negative thoughts and emotions. When we do that, we clear the path for manifestations to occur.

Life is interesting. Every day brings something new. And every day can bring new negative emotions, or feelings we don't prefer. *It's my intention to help you reframe this quickly and not spend too much time diagnosing negative emotions.*

It's easy for us, as humans, to get bogged down in thinking. As my mentor often reminds me, "de-intellectualize." Stop thinking so hard. You don't have to unravel everything, just look at it differently. This can be done in seconds.

There are entire books on reframing. But the only thing I want you to focus on is diffusing extremes, finding evidence of the opposite, and different interpretations.

When you diffuse extremes, you are becoming more aware of what you're feeding your subconscious mind and increasing what I call *positive mind food.*

When you can find evidence of the opposite, you can see something from a different perspective that is actually useful to you.

We are still in the awareness phase of manifesting, shifting into the alignment phase. When you identify a negative thought, you are becoming aware of what is getting in the way of progress rather than pushing for progress unconscious of the big pink elephant. It's really a waste of time and energy.

When you reframe a negative thought, you are releasing it to become more aligned with what you want to manifest. Essentially, you're releasing the sinkers on the line, so the cork can go back to what it naturally does—float.

Let's look at the negative thought of *None of what I'm doing is working.* Whether you are shifting to a higher level in your business or at the beginning of your business journey, this thought is a common one.

First, I want you to diffuse extremes:

Is NOTHING working? Or are some things working a little, but overall, not as much as you would prefer?

Have you looked at the data to see what is actually happening?

What results did you expect to see from the specific actions you have taken?

See how we begin to diffuse the situation a little. We don't need to spend a whole lot of time here, just take some of the extreme assumptions out of the statement.

Next, ask yourself, what are three pieces of evidence that support the opposite of NOTHING working? Here are more than three examples for me, personally.

I actually got a reply to an email I sent the other day, by someone who wanted more info on my program.

My posts are getting a lot of views.

I'm posting everywhere, so I'm increasing visibility, which is good.

I had one questionnaire come in last week that looked like it was from someone more aligned with my new target audience.

I'm generating more revenue, even if I'm completely maxed out, it tells me that people want what I have to offer.

I actually got a call booked last week, so it worked THAT time.

Bonus technique: If you really want to dig down deep and release a core belief, try this:

Identify an event or series of events that created the belief we've identified in chapter five. *Remember* the vibrational sinker? Usually, a memory will pop up quickly that is related to that belief.

Once you have an event or series of events related to the formation of this belief (your interpretation), I want you to write down at least 4 other possible interpretations of the event.

Here's an example:

I was often told that I was lazy as a child. There are several events where I can remember that label hurting and making me feel not good enough. *This was my interpretation.*

If I look at these events with the intent of listing other possible interpretations, this is what my list might look like:

1. I was lazy. But that's not necessarily a bad thing, it doesn't make me bad.

2. The adults in my life did not recognize that I was introverted, more contemplative, and found more enjoyment in other things.

3. The adults in my life did not have the knowledge or understanding of how to motivate a child to engage in specific activities.

4. The adults in my life felt frustrated by the activity at hand and some of that frustration was directed towards me.

5. The adults in my life could not see that I was overwhelmed and interpreted that as laziness.

You can see from this list that the belief that I am not good enough because I am lazy doesn't really hold water anymore. I can let it go.

We could go on and on, but you get the idea

And get ready to move on. We don't need to unpack everything, just simply let it go.

Here are some common things I hear in my work with clients and how we reframe (diffuse and find evidence that supports the opposite).

I was told that you have to work hard to get what you want.

Has anyone ever, in the history of the world, gotten what they wanted without working hard?

Well, yes.

There you go, that's evidence that you don't have to work hard to get what you want. You choose.

I don't think I have what it takes to build a business.

What do you define as "what it takes?"

Knowledge, taking action, and not stopping.

Can you gain knowledge?

Yes

Are you taking action?

Yes

Can you keep going? Or have you ever not stopped doing something till you reached the goal?

Yes, and yes, I have.

I am afraid that I won't be able to do this (business).

Does any part of this feel unsafe?

I don't know, I'm not sure.

How about being on social media?

No, I feel uncomfortable with that.

Do you know that thousands of people are reunited with loved ones because of social media? Seems like it can be safe.

Yeah, that's true.

I can never hold on to money.

Never? As in you've never held on to money even for a day.

That's not true, I have.

What would be an acceptable time period to consider "holding on" to money consistently?

I want to be successful, but I don't know what to do.

What does success mean to you?

Having a business that is making lots of money and attracting lots of clients.

Success is a feeling, not a thing. Many people have what you just defined as successful, but they're miserable. Is that what you want?

No, not at all.

Do you think it might help to feel what you want now, feel successful now, so you know what you want as you move forward?

Yes, of course.

I need clients to start showing up NOW, I need money NOW. I don't have time to wait anymore.

If I could tell you that your business would take off on a specific date in the future, but it's going to happen because of all the momentum you've built around it between now and then—would you stop working on it because it's not NOW?

No, of course not.

Is this the work that you feel called to do?

Yes, it's all I want to do.

If it's that important, can you see it as something you never stop working at?

Yes, I can.

So, if it's just a matter of time because you're doing all the right things, is this work that you're called to do and all you want to do worth waiting for?

Yes, it is.

From a vibrational perspective, the only time it takes for clients to start coming in is the time it takes for you to be in the vibration of or feeling of clients coming in. Are you feeling that right now?

No, I'm not.

Can you focus on that feeling and work on increasing it?

Yes.

Mantra Moment

I am capable.

When I work with clients on a deeper level, we can go into the vibration of what you'd prefer to feel, have, or become and use that to begin to elevate your state of mind and increase your vibrational frequency around the topic.

One of my clients recently spent an hour with me reframing beliefs and perspectives around going out on her own. She was leaving a company she'd been with for a while and was terrified that she wouldn't make enough money. After reframing and helping her to see how to elevate her state of mind to match the vibrational frequency of what she wanted to experience instead, she achieved incredible things.

She got several new clients and started a waiting list. All of this happened within just a few weeks (less than 30 days), and she was elated.

The process works if you follow it.

Exercise: Let the Cork Float (Return to your innate manifesting abilities.)

You can go through this exercise here in the book or use the worksheets included in the bonus resources. You can download the bonus resources at 7minuteshiftextras.com.

Practice reframing. Go back through this chapter to complete the exercise.

Go through a couple of conversations with yourself. If you can, speak out loud as you go. Or write it all down. Don't overthink it and just go with whatever comes up.

_____

_____

_____

_____

_____

_____

_____

Chapter Recap:

1. Don't forget to breathe.

2. The nature of the Universe is creation, growth, expansion (That's you!).

3. If a perspective isn't helping you, choose one that does.

4. The process works if you follow it.

"Follow your bliss, and the universe will open doors where there were only walls."

—Joseph Campbell

CHAPTER 7
The 7-Minute Shift

Step 4: My Proven Hack for Fueling Manifestations in Your Business
Exercise: Borrowing Joy
(Call up the key to manifesting results in a split second.)

If I asked you if you could think of something that would bring your mood down right now, could you do it?

Most would say, "Well yeah, I've got about a million things I think of that will do that."

My response is—if it's that easy to think of something that will bring your mood down, it's that easy to think of something that will bring your mood up. If you don't feel like you have a million things that will elevate your mind, you've got some work to do because whatever plenitude exists for the negative exists equally for the positive.

If you can shift your state of mind to the negative quickly, you can shift your state of mind to the positive quickly, and THAT, my dear, raises your vibration.

This is step 4 of The 7-Minute Shift where you learn to elevate your mind. One of my favorite things to say is: *Elevate your mind and the rest follows.*

Myself and my clients experience proof of this every single day. Just a couple days ago, I was feeling a little down. No real reason why, just woke up that way (not unusual for me). So, I went through the 7-Minute Shift, and throughout the day, I practiced more.

There are advanced methods I teach my clients that go beyond The 7-Minute Shift that I practice regularly. I did this throughout my day, and within 24 hours, I had two new clients. I wasn't necessarily asking for new clients, but the vibration I was shifting to was of course a higher vibration, so it takes everything with it as it rises.

> **Side Note:** When you focus on raising your vibration around a specific topic, it will raise your vibration across the board, and it's not surprising to see other areas of your life reflect it.

My mentor taught me that you don't have to focus on 10 different vibrational topics for 10 different desires. You can if you want to, but it is not necessary, especially if you're finding it difficult. Sometimes I do it just for the fun of it though. *It's like vibrational exercise.*

To be fair, I have to say that every single step of the 7-Minute Shift raises your vibration or contributes to raising your vibrational frequency. This step, in particular, focuses on a tactic that you will feel instantly.

I call step 4 Borrowing Joy or Borrowing a Memory.

You have done steps 1–3: you know what's bugging you, what perspective is in the way, and you've found evidence against it and reframed. Now, it's time for step 4, choosing how you would prefer to feel and feeling it.

What's your preference?

We'll stick with the example of not having any clients. So, if you're feeling down because you don't have any clients yet, at this step, you're going to choose how you'd prefer to feel instead.

How about feeling…

Incredibly appreciative for all the clients you're going to have?

Full of excitement for your very first client who is on the way?

Full of excitement for the new client at your new price point headed in your direction?

Or, it can simply be…

I prefer to feel at ease and happy because I have plenty of clients.

Does it feel like too far of a stretch? Take it down a notch if you're having difficulty. Try focusing on something that isn't directly related to the lack of clients, but something that still excites you:

I want to feel excited and motivated. That new recipe I found for paella yesterday, that's got me excited and motivated to cook something new!

I just saw one of my fave urban paranormal fiction writers just released a new book that got me excited and motivated to read for a while. (Ok, that slipped out of my own mind, lol)

I just read an article about how this guy started his business with zero money and brought in $2 million in revenue in less than five years—that makes me super hopeful.

After spending the day outside in my garden and walking my land, I have this sense of peace and that everything will be okay. I'm happy.

If you're really feeling low and even that's a struggle, just try to identify a simple emotion that you'd rather feel, like:

Happy

Successful

Proud

Energized

Now, take a moment to recall a memory of a time when you felt that way. Doesn't matter what the memory is in relation to, we're just going to borrow the joy from it.

A memory I often call up is one about my dog, Ichabod.

He's a huge Italian mastiff. *Beautiful and well…afraid.* He's filled with fear over wheeled things, people, unfamiliar environments, and basically anything that changes.

He's been that way since we got him at eight weeks old. We didn't recognize it till he was about four or five months old, and despite our every effort to help him (think puppy school, puppy playdates, even a dog behaviorist and supplements), he never changed.

If a friend came over, Ichabod (there is power in names apparently), would tremble and pee all over the floor.

It was and is heartbreaking to see. Although now, he has a big, fenced yard and doesn't have to deal with what triggers him too often, he still struggles from time to time.

To get back to the point of the story, we got Ichabod a friend. She's a hound mix and her name is Ruby Lou. She is wonderful and shows Ichabod what it's like to be a calm, centered dog. He loves her, I'm certain of it. And they play constantly.

When I see him running full out in the yard because she's chasing him, I swear he has a smile on his face. His ears are flying backwards from the speed of his running and his big tongue lolls to one side. His eyes are filled with excitement, and in this moment, he is not afraid, and he is so, so happy.

THAT fills me with ecstatic joy. When I need to, *I can pull up this memory and leverage it to create instant joy and happiness.*

Then, I pull in what I want to see in my business reality. Get it? It's so much easier than trying to fake it or create the feeling of joy out of nothing.

Just borrow from a silly memory. Don't make it complicated.

That's it. *Step 4 is easy peasy, fun, and all about raising your vibration.*

Emotions of joy, happiness, love, and bliss are all high on the vibrational frequency scale. As you train yourself to get to this state faster and faster, the more you stay at a high vibrational frequency. And the more you will manifest, more clients, income, and ease in your business.

Mantra Moment

I can find happiness anywhere.

Remember I mentioned that it is not uncommon for me to wake up in a down mood? There were large periods of my life that I struggled with negative emotions *all the time*. If you knew me then, you probably would not have noticed it. I tried to project differently on the outside. But on the inside, I struggled. A lot.

It was really a matter of training myself. I even apply more advanced techniques these days to prevent waking up with a down mood.

But sometimes, when I am working too much without taking enough breaks to step away from it all, I lapse a little. It's ok. We're all different, and we all have patterns and habits to break and create.

It doesn't take me long to turn it all around and let the cork float.

Exercise: Borrowing Joy (Call up the key to manifesting results in a split second.)

You can go through this exercise here in the book or use the worksheets included in the bonus resources. You can download the bonus resources at 7minuteshiftextras.com.

Make a list of all the negative feelings you have around your business. No one will see this, so just let everything out that has ever darkened your mind, no matter how crazy you think it sounds.

Next to each negative feeling, I want you to write how you'd prefer to feel. Narrow this down to one word.

Negative feeling	How you'd prefer to feel
1.	
2.	
3.	
4.	
5.	
6.	
7.	
8.	
9.	
10.	
11.	
12.	
13.	
14.	
15.	

Can you recall a time when you felt each of these? Write the memory down for each preferred feeling. Now you can access the positive feelings even faster.

Preferred feeling	Memory of preferred feeling

You're such a powerful manifestor.

Chapter Recap:

1. Positive feelings are just as easy to access as negative feelings.
2. Elevate your mind, the rest follows.
3. There are advanced practices beyond The 7-Minute Shift that I teach (oooh…aren't you curious?)
4. Choose how you prefer to feel.
5. Borrow joy (by pulling up a memory that gave you the feeling you'd prefer to feel).
6. I appreciate you.

"Our minds influence the key activity of the brain, which then influences everything; perception, cognition, thoughts and feelings, personal relationships; they're all a projection of you."

—Deepak Chopra

CHAPTER 8
The 7-Minute Shift

Step 5: The Crazy Visual That Makes Your Brain Fall in Love With Your Goals
Exercise: The Eyes of You 2.0

I once had the strangest dream. Ok, I often have strange dreams, but THIS dream circles back in my mind all the time. I will preface this story by saying that I was seeing an acupuncturist at the time, and after telling him about this series of dreams that led up to the one I'm about to share, he took me off of the supplements he had me taking (LOL).

I walked through the front door of an old white farmhouse. It was very large. The house was empty, but I remember the very worn hardwood floors because my footsteps echoed loudly. There were large windows in every room, and the sun was beaming through brightly.

I went from room to room—I knew where I was going. There was no furniture, and the walls were stark white. As I walked into the last room, my perspective immediately shifted to that of the little girl sitting in the corner of the room.

She was not alone.

She and her companion were giggling quietly and facing the corner as if to hide a secret.

And her friend was an Ewok. Yes, as in *Star Wars*.

This Ewok was giggling over the same thing as her. In his little furry hands was a small chocolate egg.

You know the ones you get at Easter that are wrapped in different colored foil and come in a bag? Well, me (as the little girl) and this Ewok (I don't remember his name), were giggling over the fact that it was so hard to get the darn foil off of those little chocolate eggs.

We had chocolate all over our fingers but didn't care because occasionally, we'd actually get all the foil off and eat one!

It was bright, peaceful, and our soft giggles echoed throughout the empty house. There was a silliness and lightness to our predicament or secret, however you want to see it. And while the dream was so very strange, the emotions from it stay with me to this day.

I share this because I often think of myself as that little girl and how carefree she was, giggling and enjoying the day. Even though she was struggling with something, she wasn't alone, and she didn't let it frustrate her. She was free. She was happy, delighting in the simplest and silliest thing.

And she had the company of a fictional being (some may debate me on this) who was enjoying the situation just as much as she was. Her imagination or creation was vivid.

In the past, there were times when I wanted to be that little girl.

She was free. She was not weighed down by anything or riddled with worry. My longing to be that little girl highlighted a very important thing—how I viewed myself (then) or the self-image I held.

It brought light to the default self-image.

I did not view myself as lighthearted, happy, or free. And as long as I did not view myself as those things, I could not be those things.

How we see ourselves is the underlying current in our vibrational frequency.

So, I ask, how do you see yourself?

One good way to tell is to run this little experiment:

Next time you are out running errands and have to walk any distance, walk as if you have everything you want in your business. I mean EVERYTHING.

All the money, all the clients, all the ease.

And notice how you carry yourself. Is that different from how you carry yourself any other time?

If it isn't—amazing! You see yourself in a positive, confident, self-loving way.

If it is different, then you know you need to shift your vibration a bit to raise your default self-image. Raising your vibration will be reflected in physical ways, like how you carry yourself. Your vibration affects every aspect of your life.

If you can adopt the self-image of the version of you who has everything, then you can become that person. It only takes a little attention to the new self-image every day. If you struggle with this, don't worry… The 7-Minute Shift will help! (That's why I love it SO much.)

This step is a huge leap to manifesting more clients, income, and ease because you have to be able to BE that person who has more clients, income, and ease. *Follow me?*

Most people are not aware of this incongruence. I wasn't. Now, each time I begin to shift to an even higher vibration and new reality, I have to shift into a new self-image too (a slightly different version of me). *The one I'm working on now is a doozy!*

In step 5 of The 7-Minute Shift, you are going to visualize yourself as the person who has it all.

You can visualize the self-image as the version of you who has everything you want in your business OR you can visualize the self-image as the version of you who feels how you prefer to feel (based on the earlier steps). Try both and see which one feels better.

You can even try creating the version of you who has everything across the board—in business and life and see how that feels.

The important thing is to identify how you look, what you're wearing, the expression on your face, the way you're wearing your hair, how you carry yourself, what you're doing, etc. The more detail you can create, the better the outcome.

Hold the image of this version of you for 10–20 seconds. Use this same self-image daily.

Here's the important thing for you to understand: If you don't address your default self-image, any forward momentum, at some point, will snap back like a rubber band because your self-image is not congruent with the version of you in the reality you want to create.

Secretly, I admit that I sometimes bring the spirit of me as that little girl eating chocolate eggs with the Ewok into the version of myself who has it all.

Because she is happy and free.

Mantra Moment
I am happy and free.

PS: here are some differences I have noticed in the new versions of me that I visualize:

She's thinner and more fit (I'm currently down 10 lbs. and getting stronger).

She holds herself differently. Her shoulders are relaxed.

She has a soft smile that is confident and full of knowing.

She has an aura of confidence and ease and grace.

She enjoys every moment because she's figured it out.

She is calm.

Here's the bonus benefit of visualizing your 2.0 self every day—the new self-image acts as an anchor that you are drawn to. You'll find that you will become that version of yourself.

Exercise: The Eyes of You 2.0

You can go through this exercise here in the book or use the worksheets included in the bonus resources. You can download the bonus resources at 7minuteshiftextras.com.

I have another exercise I want you to do in preparation for getting really good at The 7-Minute Shift. This will help you feel more of the version of you that is needed in order to manifest everything you desire in your business.

Building upon the exercise earlier, once you have that version of you created, I want you to do one more thing. Look at the world around you through the eyes of your new self-image. What does the version of you who has it all see around you?

Go further:

What do you hear?

Are you tasting anything?

What can feel on your skin?

How do things around you feel when you touch them?

How do you see the world?

How do you see the person getting irritated in the line at the grocery store?

How do you feel about the things the current you worries about?

Create such a strong persona for this new self-image that you can quickly call it up every day during The 7-Minute Shift.

You are literally stepping into a version of you that already exists and choosing that version's experiences. *This still blows my mind.*

_____

_____

_____

_____

_____

_____

_____

_____

_____

_____

_____

_____

_____

Chapter Recap:

1. Be careful with spleen supplements — apparently, they can make you dream vividly.

2. Discover your default self-image (so you can shift it if necessary).

3. The default self-image is a good indicator of anything going on at the vibrational level.

4. To manifest the results you want in your business, you have to see yourself as the person or version of you who is experiencing those results.

5. Without an upgraded self-image, any forward momentum will snap back like a rubber band.

Surprise Bonus #3: I'm sharing three meditations to help you with You 2.0. Just go to 7minuteshiftextras.com to watch it, it's free.

"You cannot perceive what you are not in the vibration of."

—Darryl Anka

CHAPTER 9

The 7-Minute Shift

Step 6: Discover The Everyday Things That Can Raise Your Vibrational Frequency to Match Success
Exercise: Vibrational Elevators Hiding in Plain Sight

Dear You,

I wish I could meet you in person. I'd give you a hug and tell you how in awe I am of your courage to step into some of the greatest work you'll ever do on yourself.

Creating the vision for and bringing to life the business you dream of will challenge you deeply, personally, and emotionally.

I am in awe of you because I know the journey. And I am humbled by your decision.

I wish I could sit with you over a warm cup of coffee and laugh about all the mental acrobatics we put ourselves through to do what we came here to do. I'd tell you that your decision to enter this physical reality and experience being human is THE distraction...that your dreams are real and became real the moment you took a breath.

You are an expression of the force that creates. The catch is, you are self-aware, and that is a massive distraction.

When you get stuck in being self-aware, you are more reactive because you are getting pulled into emotions generated from things like what your family thinks of you, what others will say about failing, or what you perceive as your shortcomings.

Self-awareness is a double-edged sword. It takes away from your instincts and intuition. I believe being balanced between the three is another key to manifesting with ease. I believe it is the way we are meant to be.

Everything you want to be, you already are. You came here as a creator of worlds, but the messy emotions of your human-ness made you forget.

I wish I could walk beside you as you shape your reality and watch each step unfold in real time, beautifully crafting your business as you go. You don't chase it, you step into it, that's what I love about you.

I know you will sometimes feel that you don't have what it takes or that you're not good enough or deserving of all the success. *You'll seek validation and certainty.*

Perfection doesn't become flawed simply because it enters physical reality.

If you're just beginning your business...you'll feel vulnerable in being vulnerable. You'll be split between being visible and not wanting anyone to see you. You'll fear being judged, or getting it wrong, or repeating patterns, or failing, or having to make decisions you don't feel equipped to make.

Breathe. It's all just a ruse.

If you're shifting to a bigger version of you and your business, you'll feel like, w*ho am I to think I can be this or do this??* You'll worry about what has to be sacrificed or how much work needs to be done, you'll be driven to prove that you can do it all despite doubting you can deliver what you promise. You'll think others must have something you lack. You'll think you have to work harder than other people to make it all happen.

But the truth is they don't have something you lack, and the catch here is internal shifts not external effort. *Remember that.*

Mantra Moment

I am everything I need.

We are all vibration, a physical translation of beautiful information that groups together based on resonance, frequency, and feelings. All whole and complete packets of energy that is everything ever needed.

Always moving, doing, wishing.

I want to tell you how incredible it is to watch you become aware of the aspects of Self that get in the way of shaping your reality and, in a feat of mastery, operate this machine of a mind you have, directing it, leading it, you move IT out of the way (rather than the other way around).

If I could, I would walk with you, run with you, cry with you, scream and shout right alongside of you as you break through the invisible barriers you created for yourself with beliefs. The thing about invisible barriers is they don't really exist, *but you get that.*

I love what you are creating and how determined you are to bring this greatest expression of Self (your business) to fruition in order to take care of yourself and others.

You're brave. Facing Self is the ultimate test of courage. There is no greater experience. Why else would we come here?

Maybe one day, we'll meet, and we'll celebrate your expansion with such resonance that we shake the trees and feel the joy of it in our bones. *And revel in the business that is you.*

It's time for step 6. Step 6 is all about your vibrational baseline. This is where your vibration naturally sits at all times. Your perceptions, beliefs, emotions, and thoughts that are quietly hanging out in the background create this baseline.

It's not uncommon for people who have not done any of this kind of work on Self before to have a low vibrational baseline. So don't be shocked or feel discouraged if you discover your vibrational baseline is lower than you wish. Because we are going to raise it.

It is near impossible to maintain an elevated state of mind and high vibration 100% of the time. You will have moments of contrast. The trick is to keep your vibrational baseline as high as you can most of the time, so when you do fall a couple of notches on the vibrational scale, you won't fall too far.

It's like if you walked a balance beam that was only three inches off the ground. If you fall off, no big deal, you just hop back up. It doesn't take long. Before you know it, you're back at your previous level of focus.

But If that balance beam is say, 20 feet off the ground, and you fall off, you're not going to hop back up. It's going to take a while. You may not feel so good either. It will not be easy getting back up to your previous level of focus if you do at all.

The idea here is to raise your vibrational baseline with everyday things that are all around you all the time, so if you get knocked off that balance beam, it's no big deal. It won't take you long to get back to your high level of focus and an elevated mind.

Doing so helps you maintain an elevated state of mind longer, regain it faster, and eventually change your thought habits. (And manifest consistently.)

Can you see what I'm getting at?

Let's review the steps of The 7-Minute Shift so far:

1. Identify what's in the way (negative feeling).
2. Find the perspective causing the belief that's causing the feeling (and release it).
3. Find evidence to support the opposite.
4. Elevate your mind—choose how you prefer to feel.
5. Create a new self-image that feels what you prefer to feel.

And…

Raise your vibrational baseline by bringing attention to at least 3 everyday things that give you the feeling you prefer.

Example:

I prefer to feel stable and secure.

The chair I'm sitting in is very secure.

My legs are pretty stable.

The car I'm driving feels secure.

This door I'm closing and locking is very secure.

The building I'm in is stable.

I prefer to feel happy and successful.

My dog makes me feel happy.

This cup of coffee is heavenly and makes me feel happy.

I just created a new webinar, I feel pretty successful.

I just wrote another email, I feel successful.

I cleaned out my car, I feel successful.

I had a bowl of my favorite ice cream and that made me happy.

My cat's purring makes me happy.

Pulling up in my driveway and seeing lights on in my house makes me happy.

I prefer to feel confident.

I just brushed my hair, I know how to brush my hair, I'm confident in my ability to do so.

I washed dishes, I'm confident in my ability to do so.

I held a Zoom call, I'm confident in my ability to do so.

I got the kids dressed, fed, and to school, I'm confident in my ability to do so.

I got myself dressed, fed, and to work, I'm confident in my ability to do so (lol).

I made a decision to say "no" to doing something that I really didn't want to do, I'm confident in my ability to do so.

I typed a document today, I'm confident in my ability to do so.

I prefer to feel free.

I'm free to talk or not talk today.

I'm free to eat or not eat today.

I'm free to wear my hair however I want.

I'm free to wear whatever color socks I want.

I'm free to take a deep breath.

I'm free to blink.

I'm free to smile.

As you read these examples, you may think these are ridiculously silly things, but they're not. You're bringing attention to things and actions that give you the feeling you prefer and acknowledging that you experience these preferred feelings multiple, if not hundreds of, times a day.

Remember, the cork always floats. When you take a moment to identify how you'd prefer to feel, your inner guidance is going to always go for what allows the cork to float. So, naturally, you're going to raise your vibration in the process. As you understand this more and more and become really good at changing how you feel quickly, you'll get just how powerful you are as a creator.

You are powerful.

You can choose at any moment what you prefer, what you want to create, and who you are.

Exercise: Vibrational Elevators Hiding in Plain Sight

You can go through this exercise here in the book or use the worksheets included in the bonus resources. You can download the bonus resources at 7minuteshiftextras.com.

Make a list of 10 ways you prefer to feel. For each feeling, write three everyday things that give you this feeling. Remember that the everyday things are often things we take for granted, so really look at your daily routine and how everything that is a part of it makes you feel.

Now you'll have a nice bank to mentally pull from during your daily 7-Minute Shift. Soon, you're going to be able to go through The 7-Minute Shift in your head very quickly. These written exercises will give you what you need to be able to do that.

How I prefer to feel	Three everyday things that give me this feeling

Chapter Recap:

1. You are a creator of worlds.

2. We all have a vibrational baseline.

3. Your perceptions, beliefs, emotions, and thoughts create your vibrational baseline.

4. Raise your vibrational baseline throughout the day, so you don't fall so far when you have a bad day.

5. Knowing how you prefer to feel and the everyday things that give you this feeling help you maintain an elevated state of mind longer, regain it faster, and change your thought habits.

"People love chopping wood. In this activity one immediately sees results."

—Albert Einstein

CHAPTER 10
The 7-Minute Shift

Step 7: The Send Button for Your Business Results
Exercise: Hit the "Send Button" for Your Business Manifestations

Every step of the 7-Minute Shift is designed for you to experience immediate results. Whether you feel different, gain a different perspective, or even have an ah-ha moment, it's immediate. We all love immediate results. You get to have immediate results every single day while also building powerful momentum for shifting your reality!

Now, it's time to integrate! Every process has a send button—some final action or step that completes it or sets it in motion.

The way we set The 7-Minute Shift into motion is by giving the brain a visual and the physical body an action that makes it real. This step can be so effective that people report feeling a difference immediately. They actually feel something shift internally as do I. That's what we're after!

But if you don't feel anything when you start, don't worry, continue on (you're doing it right).

One of the best teachings I ever received was about making a decision. The teaching focused on how simple making a decision can be with anything. If you want to feel differently, then decide right here and now, in this moment, how you want to feel. It must be so final that you feel the decision deep in your bones.

If we learn to manage the brain that we have (rather than let the brain manage us), we can effectively tell the brain what is now real and in effect.

Physical movement helps to make this happen.

Now, we're not doing anything crazy here, just something quick, small, and easy, so we can solidify the previous six steps. Think of it as anchoring the shift every single day. Here are some ways you can solidify those previous steps.

1. Locate It

Identify where you feel the positive emotion in your body. Maybe you feel it in your chest or your stomach, or it rolls through your body like a wave of electricity. Maybe you feel the buzzing of emitting a high vibration? Relax and feel where you feel these feelings in your body.

Imagine you draw a circle around that part of your body. (My mentor draws a frame around it.)

Take the shape that now outlines the location of the positive feeling in your body, and physically push it farther away with your hands. Then physically pull it closer with your hands. This is necessary to make a connection in the brain that you're actually changing something. Which feels better? Closer or farther away?

For example, I identify the center of my chest as the positive emotion location. I physically point to the center of my chest and draw a circle around it. Then I move my hands forward pulling the circle with them. I like the visual of a glowing orb, so I envision that. As I pull this glowing orb towards me, I feel MORE positive emotions, so I stick with this direction. This may be different tomorrow, but for now closer feels better.

Next, expand it or condense it. Make it bigger or make it smaller—which feels better?

I like to expand the orb until I can step into it. And I do. I literally take two steps forward as I step into this orb of positive emotions that encapsulates everything I've created in my 7-Minute Shift.

Here are more ways I might integrate my 7-Minute Shift:

2. Become It

I imagine the version of me that I identified earlier in the process. I have a really solid vision of this version of me now, so I can call that up quickly. I see her just a few steps ahead of me. I take two or three steps forward (literally) and step into her, merging into one person.

3. Activate It

Imagine that you have a secret panel on the inside of your left forearm. When you press it, the panel opens and there's a digital screen. You see the words "Install Update?" There's a green button that says "Activate." Press it. Take a moment to feel this upgrade move throughout your body.

You can walk through a beam of light, flip a switch, jump from one reality to another, walk through a doorway, snap, clap, whatever you want to do that involves some movement and a decisive action.

That's your "submit button" and the way to finalize your shift every single day.

Even though I've taken a handful of chapters to explain The 7-Minute Shift to you, once you go through it a few times, it really becomes quick and easy.

These 7 minutes a day (or less) do two things that are probably the most important things you'll ever do for yourself:

1. Shift any limiting beliefs/thoughts/emotions out of the way of what you want.

2. Build your innate manifesting abilities, so momentum builds, and you begin to experience manifestations of the results you want to see, day after day, after day. (That's the secret to manifesting consistently—build the momentum for it *consistently.*)

This brings me to yet another really important point. We've been in the Information Age for quite some time. When the internet connected us to everything, to the point of being able to "Google" any question and get a multitude of answers, we reached the height of the Information Age, so far at least.

Then we shifted. We shifted into the Exponential Growth Age. You can see evidence of this all around you. Crypto, finances, social movements, technology, everywhere you look, you can see evidence of exponential growth.

You and I are in this too. Your business is in the Exponential Growth Age and therefore can tap into exponential growth.

It requires exponential growth of you, the human being. Learning to use your mind differently is a start. Learning to manage your state of mind in every moment AND harness your ability to manifest IS the key to creating exponential growth for you, your business, and your life.

Now, I'm not referencing a purely mathematical definition of exponential growth but rather a more general one that says the larger something gets, the faster it grows. So, when applying The 7-Minute Shift, as you begin to experience more and more results, the faster those results will happen.

Or, as you begin to elevate your state of mind more and more, the faster you will experience an elevated state of mind, a higher vibration, and a physical manifestation of what you desire (like a highly successful business).

The bigger your business gets using The 7-Minute Shift, the faster it grows. The more ah-ha's you have, the faster you have them. The more manifestations you create, the faster they show up.

You get the idea. It's incredible and mystical in some ways, yet logical and law.

Mantra Moment

I can create exponential growth.

Exercise: Hit the "Send Button" for Your Business Manifestations

You can go through this exercise here in the book or use the worksheets included in the bonus resources. You can download the bonus resources at 7minuteshiftextras.com.

Choose a few visualizations that pair with physical movement to use in this step from day-to-day. I personally find the visualization of the 2.0 version of me to be the most powerful. I see her in every detail and step into her. It's quick and easy.

Sometimes though, it will be more effective to use an amplification visual and physical movement—like drawing a circle around where you feel the positiveness in your body and make the circle/sphere bigger. Amplify it. *It still amazes me how you can feel this!*

If you're about to go for a walk or workout, do the 7-Minute Shift just before you begin and integrate it with your workout!

You may eventually create even more amplification and integration visuals/movements. For this exercise, simply create two. One that is a more decisive, "step into" kind of thing and one that amplifies.

_____

_____

_____

_____

_____

_____

_____

_____

_____

_____

_____

_____

_____

_____

Chapter Recap:

1. Every process has a finalization step or "send" button.

2. There's an important connection made in the brain when we physically move.

3. By doing all of this, you are moving the things out of your way that keep most people stuck for lifetimes. And you are strengthening your ability to manifest. This is the most powerful combination I know.

4. We are in the Exponential Growth Age. Tap into using your mind differently and create exponential growth for you and your business.

So here are the steps of The 7-Minute Shift:

Awareness Phase
Step 1: Detect Resistance (N)

What's in the way today?

In step 1, you bring your attention to any negative feelings, resistance, or otherwise non-serving thoughts. If, at any point during the day, a limiting or negative thought pops up, go through all of the steps again.

Step 2: Find the Vibrational Sinker (P)

What's the perspective?

In step 2, you identify the perspective that is creating the negative feeling and thought. Having this ability is an incredible growth strategy. You will have many ah-has here.

Step 3: Let the Cork Float (R)

Reframe the perspective.

While step 3 takes a little time to get really good at it, it is an invaluable skill. Some of our greatest leaders have the ability to do this instantly and move on to their next decision. This is powerful internal work that creates external results.

Alignment Phase
Step 4: Borrowing Joy (E)

Shifting your mindset.

Now you're creating new emotions, new feelings, and as a result, a new state of mind. Never skimp on this step, stay with it till you feel it.

Step 5: The Eyes of You 2.0 (S)

Visualizing your new self-image.

In all the work I've done, this is the most crucial step that I missed for years. If you're not getting anywhere or seem to snap back to an old pattern, then your self-image needs a close look. If your self-image is always of the "old" you, then new manifestations may not stick around long because there's a belief that the "old" you can't have those manifestations, whatever they are.

Create a version of you who has it all and hold that daily.

Step 6: Vibrational Elevators in Plain Sight (V)

Changing your vibrational baseline.

To actively manifest a different result in your business, like more clients, income, and ease, you have to create a vibrational frequency that matches that of more clients, income, and ease. You start by identifying how these things feel to you and experience that feeling now. Even if you're looking to shift to a new level in your business, change branding, change the level at which you work with clients, you identify that vibrational frequency first. Then shift it.

Action Phase
Step 7: Hit the Send Button (I)

Integrate it and take action.

In this final step, you are making a decision and taking physical action to integrate the brain with everything you've done so far. In addition, you are sending off the vibratory message for a specific manifestation. In this case, specific results in your business that show in the 2.0 version of you that you created. When it shows in you through your feelings and actions, it must be reflected.

As you begin to go through the 7-Minute Shift without pen and paper, it may help you to remember the steps the way I do: N.P.R.E.S.V.I.

N - Negative emotion

P - Perspective

R - Reframe

E - Elevate

S - Self-Image

V - Vibration

I - Integrate

There you have it. The 7-Minute Shift. You really can shift your business results in as little as 7 minutes a day.

SECTION III
Conclusion, Confession, and Continuation

It's inner work that upgrades you. As you upgrade, you begin to grow in exponential ways, and it is reflected everywhere "you" are applied. Anything that is an expression of you, a business, a career, a book, a family, art, your physical body, etc., will take on this exponential growth along with unbelievable manifestations.

I still have days that I say to myself, in complete awe… "This is the way it really works, we really do influence our reality." It still blows my mind.

When I began my company, ElevatedMind™, I knew with absolute certainty that it would become the foundation for unlimited success and discoveries. In the first quarter of this year, I tripled my income. Synchronicities occur on a daily basis (well, they always occur, but I now notice them on a daily basis).

I hope you do too.

"Once you make a decision, the universe conspires to make it happen."

—Ralph Waldo Emerson

CHAPTER 11
Tracking Progress & Results

Exercise: The Proof in the Pudding (Banana please)

I don't want to say goodbye. Maybe we won't. My connection to everyone who does "this" work is deep. It's like we know who "we" are and there's this incredible sense of belonging, creation, and potential. We are forever connected. (Thank you, High-Vibe Tribe.)

We are creators of worlds. And whether you know it yet or not, you are creating your world right now. *Your world includes your business.*

But we're not quite done yet. I want you to track your progress.

Exercise: The Proof in the Pudding (Banana please)

Since it doesn't make sense to complete this exercise in the workbook, you can download the complimentary guide at 7minuteshiftextras.com and use the spreadsheet and charts I created for you.

1. **SOM spreadsheet:** This allows you to track your **state of mind** every day. It's very simple in concept and takes seconds to implement. If you track your results from the time you start practicing The 7-Minute Shift, you will see a difference. This sheet will show you how your state of mind shifts AND how you're able to stay in an elevated state more consistently over time. This is what is needed to manifest. Remember, it's momentum-based and compounding. It's important that you "see" the changes.

2. **Vibrational Pie Chart:** The other tracking sheet is the **pie chart sheet**. These pie charts are blank. I suggest you make copies of this (or create your own digital version) and label them with whatever you are focusing on increasing your vibration around.

For example, if you identify on Tuesday that you have some resistance around money and you'd prefer to feel that you have a plethora of money, so much so that it's spilling over and filling your reserves…shade in your pie chart as you go through your day and give attention to that feeling.

If you can reach 70% or better, you're doing incredible. If it's less than that at the end of the day, this is a good visual to remind you that it's a choice. You can choose how you feel and bring your attention to it consistently. Try it, then see it reflected in your pie chart. Correlate manifestations of your shift with your pie chart tracking.

Tracking helps you do the thing you're tracking more and helps you elevate your mind around the thing you want to manifest because you can see the positive results occurring. You see the results, you do more, you see the results, you do more.

Confession time. I've never been one to track things. Matter of fact, I've actively resisted. I rolled my eyes at calorie tracking. I rolled my eyes at goal tracking. I rolled my eyes at routines of any sort. For years! If someone suggested I journal daily…you got it, I'd roll my eyes.

Then I had a realization and a bit of reframing. I used to say that if someone said "routine" I'd run the other way. But that is SO not true. I drink coffee every single morning. It's a routine that borders on obsession. I read certain books every single day. I check email accounts every single day. That is a lot of routines.

I track stats for my business too. I had to acknowledge that I do in fact track things and have routines. I had to dig down to the perspectives that were shaping my negative beliefs around routines and tracking. And I let them go. Because it was certainly getting in the way of where I wanted to go.

There are plenty of creative, inspiring, fun, and charismatic people in the world who track progress and create routines.

Tracking progress and creating positive routines is my way (and yours too) of creating that invisible flywheel. The more momentum I give it, the faster it will take off on its own and help me manifest more and more and more. The faster I'll see results because I see micro-results.

You get my point. You may love to track results and create routines, but if you're anything like me, my confession may help.

Mantra Moment

I am progressing toward my goals with ease.

When you begin to experience results in your business shifting in the direction you desire (and you will), I want you to take note. Revel in the feeling of it. This serves to compound the manifesting materials we use on a daily basis.

Whether you are creating your own tracking sheets or using the ones I've provided, go ahead and get it all set up. You won't track forever, but the momentum-building, motivation-inducing effects of tracking your progress and results are important in the beginning. I recommend tracking for at least 90 days.

In no time, you'll be a master of The 7-Minute Shift and step into your full potential.

Chapter Recap:

1. Use the SOM spreadsheet to track your state of mind. I recommend tracking for 90 days minimum.

2. Use the Vibrational Pie Charts to track the percentage of your attention being shifted to what you prefer.

3. Tracking progress and results does not make you nerdy and boring :) (Okay, maybe that was for me)

"*The universe is not outside of you. Look inside yourself; everything that you want, you already are.*"

—Rumi

CHAPTER 12
Advanced Work and Future Pacing

Let's fast forward a bit in the movie. Let's get to the part where you are seeing incredible results in your business. This is what happened:

You began practicing The 7-Minute Shift every single day. You noticed an immediate shift in your state of mind, and very shortly after, you began to see little shifts in your business. An opportunity showed up to be more visible. A client was referred to you. You were asked to present at an event.

This excitement and slight disbelief solidified your dedication to the daily practices. Before you knew it, you were calling up the **You 2.0** throughout the day and **Borrowing Joy** outside of your dedicated seven minutes. You noticed your state of mind tracking was showing a leveling out, which meant you were maintaining an elevated state of mind more consistently.

Then bigger shifts began to happen.

You get another client, then another, your messaging pivots and upleveling is grabbing attention. You're now working with the kind of client you have wanted to work with for so long (but hadn't been aware of). The business is picking up speed and you can feel it deep in your bones.

Each day, you're releasing resistance and negative perspectives that would have kept you stuck, but now they are simply swept away and replaced by higher vibrational frequencies. Suddenly, you realize that your income has doubled and stayed there for several months. (Whaaaat?!)

Clients are showing up everywhere, referrals, emails, social media, and in more ways you never even thought of. You bring on more help and expand your reach.

This feels so easy and natural, which brings a bit of a hiccup in trusting that this will all stay. But you know what to do—you do it every day. The 7-Minute Shift.

The strangest thing is that when a new client shows up unexpectedly, you know there will be a few more manifestations coming with it—it always seems to happen in multiples. It's exhilarating, inspiring, and downright blissful.

You want to stay in this place of mind-blowing bliss every single day (and you can).

More and more and more keeps showing up. More and more and more money, abundance, and expansion. Exponential growth is something you fully get now. As your business grows bigger, the faster it grows. And it was all in your power to create all along.

Is this how it really works? *Yes, it is.*

You feel at ease, incredibly happy, and in total awe of the experience.

Ok, pause the movie.

It's time to talk about what happens next. What do you want NOW? Have you ever thought beyond this point? Can you think bigger and bigger and bigger? Remember, you are a product of that which seeks expansion as an experience of life itself.

You are meant to want more. (Hit play again)

Client waitlists begin to form, BIG partnerships coalesce, you've hit your biggest revenue point ever, and money is showing up in large amounts, $8K, $10K, $13K, $20K, $45K and more. Sometimes, it's even a little scary how you are manifesting such results, but it's good scary.

All of these things have happened for myself and my clients. It's such an incredible life, experience, and ah-ha moment.

I invite you to go even further.

There is more. If you want to go further with this work, go to 7minuteshiftextras.com to fill out the form to request more information about the programs ElevatedMind™ has to offer.

Based on the information you provide, myself or a team member will send you details for what is relevant to where you are and where you want to be.

There are many ways you can continue this work outside of my program and coaching at ElevatedMind™. In the resources section, I've listed numerous books that have been beneficial to me. I'm certain that whatever you need to continue and deepen this work, sharpen your manifesting skills, and take your business further than ever, will present itself.

You are after all, a creator, and you create it ALL.

One last thing before I go (with tears welling up). Whatever it is that you want to create in your business, you can. If you've been at this a while and you have a successful business, but you feel stuck in your current results and you want MORE, you can shift everything till you reach the MORE you desire.

If you are simply stuck in "I don't know what to do or what I want," it's okay, you can find clarity and certainty.

My point is, it doesn't matter where you are in your business, how long you've been in business, how big or small your goals are, or whatever else you can think of. You can shift from where you are to where you want to be. *You can tap into this Age of Exponential Growth and discover your mind and capabilities in a whole new way.*

All I ask is that you be open to learning and discovering things you've never imagined.

It's not magic, but it is innate and intrinsic.

So be what you already are and create everything you desire.

Mantra Moment

I am a powerful creator.

I'll close by circling back around to the beginning: You and every other person on this planet has access to the same frequencies. We all have the same amount of time in the day. We all have the same basic thoughts. It's how we manage these thoughts that enables us to build a highly successful business. It's whether we choose to consciously manifest or not that enables us to influence our reality in the direction we desire or simply take what life (Self) throws at us.

Elevate your state of mind, the rest will follow.

Much love & manifesting.

Michelle Sera

Resources

My favorite books on manifesting and more:

Money Magic – Michelle Masters

Power Manifesting – Nick Breau

Rich as F*ck – Amanda Frances

Automatic Manifestations – Richard Dotts

Super Attractor – Gabrielle Bernstein

Bluefishing – Steve Sims

Any book or collection of writings by Neville Goddard

Thank & Grow Rich – Pam Grout

The Course in Miracles Experiment – Pam Grout

Real Magic – Dean Radin, PhD

Advanced Manifesting with Frequencies – Linda West

My Plan for Living to Be 156 – Dan Sullivan

The Creation Frequency – Mike Murphy, Jack Canfield

Parallel Universes of Self – Frederick E. Dodson

The Matrix Energetics Experience – Richard Bartlett, DC ND

Reality Transurfing: Steps I-V – Vadim Zeland

Re-Create Your Life – Marty Lefkoe

Other businesses you should know about:

Jessica Wright

Wright Life Coaching

Leading restless and bored souls (who want more) to choose a life of meaning and authenticity without losing everything and everyone they care about.

http://www.jessicawright.online/

https://www.instagram.com/jwrightlife/

http://www.linkedin.com/in/jessicarwright/

Tina DeMarco

Writing coach & copywriter

Blue Coat Writers Group

https://www.memoirmuse.com/

Maxine Loader

7-Figure FB Ads Strategist

Helping 6 figure coaches scale to 7 figures and beyond using Facebook ads.

https://www.instagram.com/maxineloader

Moira Sutton

Author, Speaker, Lifestyle Coach, Empowerment Mentor, Spiritual Teacher, Host and Producer of the Heart Soul Wisdom Podcast.

https://www.moirasutton.com/

podcast.heartsoulwisdom.com/

http://www.linkedin.com/in/moira-sutton-9b972a1/

http://www.facebook.com/CreatetheLifeyouLove1/

Kent Petersen

Breakthrough & Epiphany Coach

Facebook group: Manifesting Mastermind

ManifestingGeniusCoaching@gmail.com

www.ingramcontent.com/pod-product-compliance
Lightning Source LLC
Chambersburg PA
CBHW082147120626
46553CB00010B/2804